The History *of* Mar Yahballaha & Rabban Sawma

The History *of* Mar Yahballaha & Rabban Sawma

Translated by
Pier Giorgio Borbone and Laura E. Parodi

Edited and Annotated by
Thomas A. Carlson

Hackett Publishing Company
Indianapolis

Printed in the United States of America

29 28 27 26 1 2 3 4 5 6 7

For further information, please address

Hackett Publishing Company, Inc.
P.O. Box 44937
Indianapolis, Indiana 46244-0937

www.hackettpublishing.com

Hackett Publishing Company, Inc. | Independent | Employee Owned

Cover design by E. L. Wilson
Interior design by Laura Clark
Composition by Aptara, Inc.

Library of Congress Control Number: 2025933571

ISBN-13: 978-1-64792-237-5 (pbk.)
ISBN-13: 978-1-64792-243-6 (PDF ebook)
ISBN-13: 978-1-64792-244-3 (epub)

The paper used in this publication meets the minimum requirements of American National Standard for Information Sciences—Permanence of Paper for Printed Library Materials, ANSI Z39.48–1984.

∞

Contents

Genealogies vi

Maps viii

Acknowledgments xi

Introduction 1

***The History of Mar Yahballaha and Rabban Sawma* 35**

Glossary 153

Select Bibliography 157

Image Credits 161

Index 163

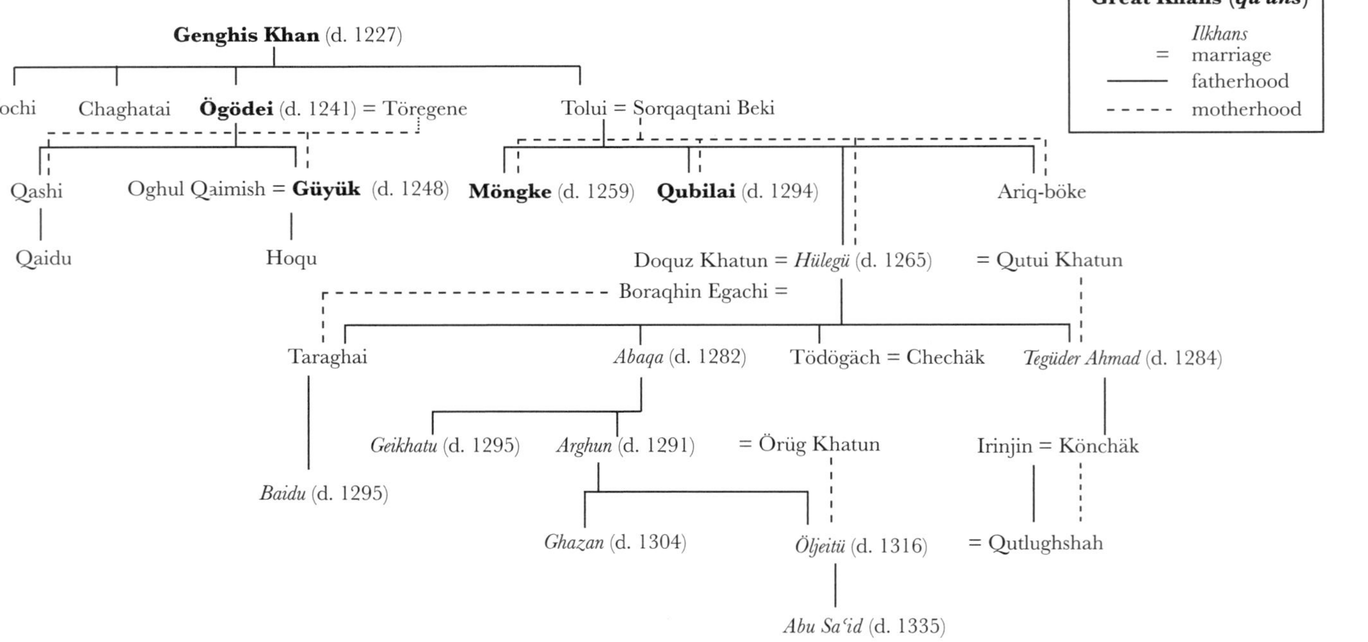

Great Khans and Ilkhans.

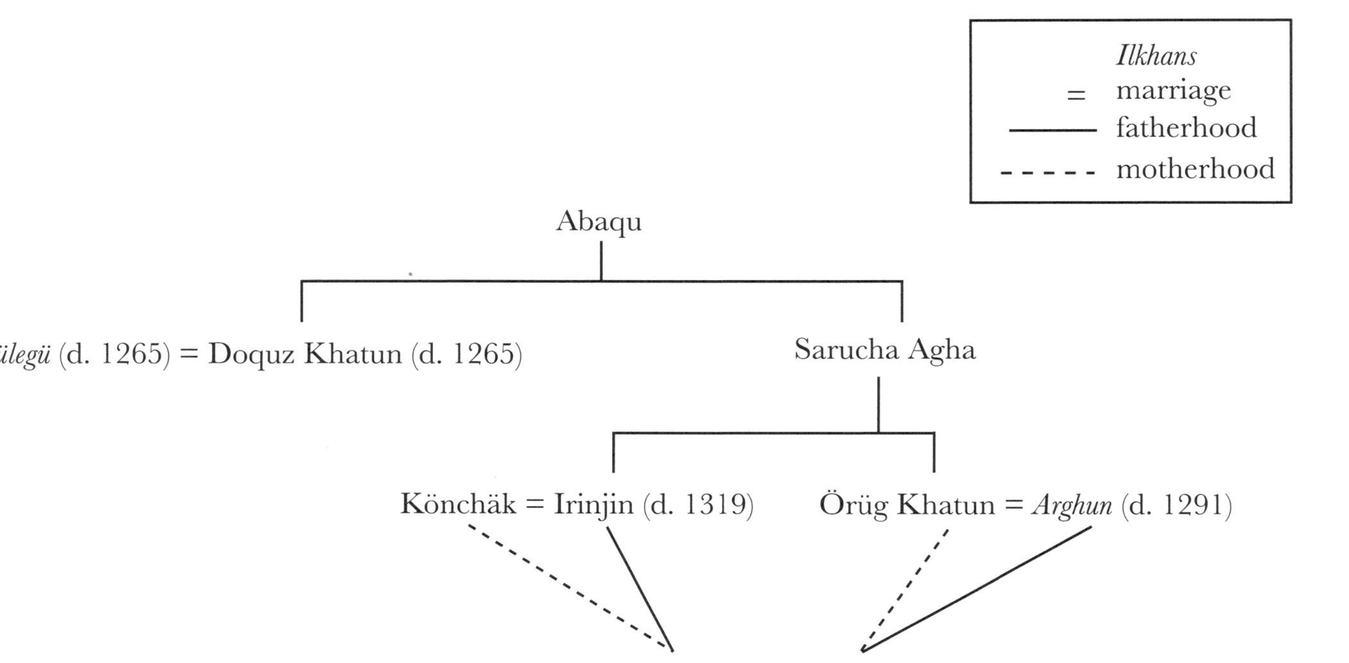

Keraits intermarried with the Ilkhans.

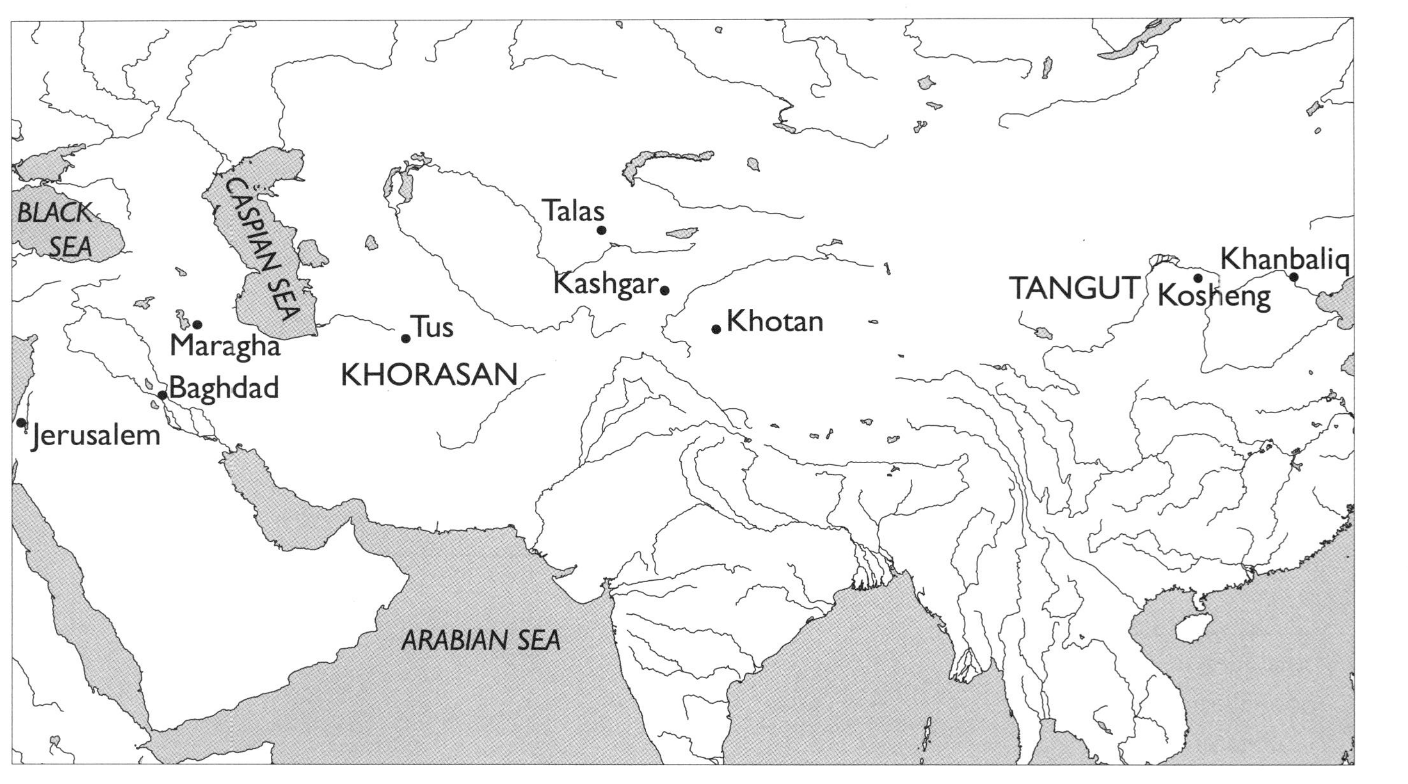

A journey across Asia: the route taken by Rabban Sawma and Rabban Mark from northern China to the Middle East.

The Middle East during the Mongol period.

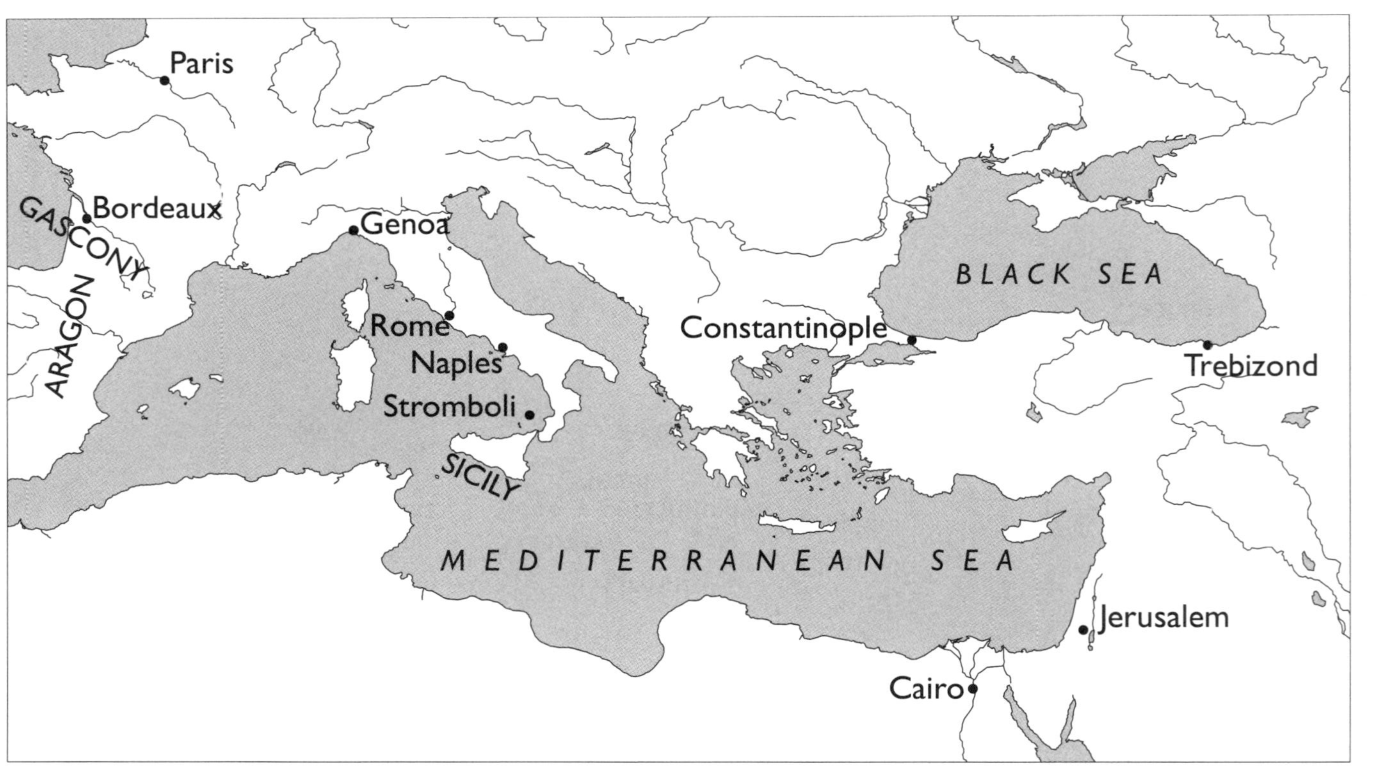

Rabban Sawma's Embassy to Europe.

ACKNOWLEDGMENTS

The idea for this project came from Rick Todhunter, whom I also thank for tolerating my many questions and suggestions. My earlier work on the source was prompted by invitations from Foteini Spingou and David Thomas, which prepared the way for me to work on this volume. Late stages of work on the book were undertaken at the Institute for Advanced Study in Princeton, New Jersey, with the support of a Patricia Crone membership.

I appreciate the encouragement to work on this text from Pier Giorgio Borbone and Joel Walker. I am grateful to many colleagues for answering questions I had as I worked on this text, including Mark Dickens, Gianmaria Gianazza, Jan van Ginkel, Giovanni Gomiero, Emily Graham, Stefan Kamola, John Romano, and Dietmar Winkler. Thanks are due to Harmony McSorley and Jackson Moore for reading the initial translation for clarity and for providing input. I thank Mary Carlson for assistance improving the clarity and style of my prose, and technological assistance with preparing the index. Two anonymous reviewers provided useful suggestions for improving the Introduction and translation. Remaining mistakes are due to my own stubbornness.

Thomas A. Carlson

April 2025

Introduction

Marco Polo was not the only traveler to cross the width of Eurasia in the 1200s. At the very moment when Marco Polo was accompanying his father and uncle from Venice to China, two other travelers (who were more important in their time) were moving in the opposite direction. They were eastern Turks, born in China, and traveling as Christian pilgrims with the goal of reaching Jerusalem and the holy places there. They never reached that destination, but instead they played key roles in Eurasian geopolitics at a moment of rapid change. The older of the two, known as Rabban Sawma,[1] was sent as an ambassador by the Mongol rulers of Iran to the courts of European Christendom, meeting the kings of France and England as well as the new pope in Rome and the Byzantine emperor in Constantinople, seeking to broker a military alliance to recapture Jerusalem from the Mamluk Empire of Egypt. His younger fellow traveler was selected to lead their eastern Christian denomination, known in English as the "Church of the East," with its headquarters in Baghdad, under the name of Mar Yahballaha III.[2] As Marco Polo made his way back home to Venice, Rabban Sawma passed away at a good old age, and Yahballaha III corresponded with the pope and western kings, as he personally led the largest Christian community in Iraq and Iran through the shifting conditions of Mongol rule, during the period in which many members of the Mongol government converted to Islam. Unlike Marco Polo, neither of these eastern Turks returned home. This is the story of those two travelers and Christian leaders from East Asia who traveled westward, almost Marco Polo in reverse.

---

1. "Rabban" is a title of respect, literally "our chief."

2. "Yahballaha" means "God gave," similar to the Greek name Theodore (i.e., "gift of God"), while "Mar" is a title of honor meaning "my lord."

This primary source is unique in many ways. We have many Latin European accounts of travels to Asia during the medieval period, but this may be the only text authored by an Asian traveler describing what he saw in Latin Europe. Out of the dozens of people who were sent as Mongol ambassadors to the popes and kings of Christendom, Rabban Sawma is the only one whose travel account is preserved, providing a unique outsider's perspective on high medieval Europe, including, among other things, an early description of the University of Paris. At a moment when the Roman church hierarchy was seeking to centralize control and root out what they considered "heresy," they welcomed Rabban Sawma with curiosity and exchanged the sacraments with a church leader from the East whom their doctrine would label as heretical. His skillful politeness enabled him to avoid contentious theological disputes, which were at that time being used so aggressively by Latin inquisitors against Jews and "heretics," without compromising his own views.

Beyond Europe, this text also reveals both the opportunities and tribulations of individuals subject to the rule of the Mongol Empire of Genghis Khan. It describes some of the inner workings of that empire, alongside its diplomatic successes and failures, from the perspective of someone who had access to the Mongol royal encampment but was not writing to curry favor with the ruler. The account also details the complex relationships between Christians and Muslims in the Middle East during a period of religious transformation, as the Mongol ruling class converted to Islam and cemented the ascendancy of that religion from Anatolia to Central Asia. This unique primary source was written by a contemporary during the lifetimes of the two main characters and shortly after their deaths. The entire text is presented here, rather than only the diplomatic mission to Europe or the later Christian-Muslim strife and negotiations, in the hopes that the whole text, seen together, will provide a fuller picture than carving it up. But to understand the text, it is first necessary to know something of the political and religious context in which the events unfolded, as well as how the text took shape and was transmitted to us seven centuries later.

The Mongol Moment in World History

Some measure of how the world became interconnected as a result of Genghis Khan's conquests might be seen in the increasing number of names known across the width of Eurasia. Although it is difficult to prove, it is likely that the first person whose name was known from England to China was Jesus, since Christian missionaries from Persia entered China in the mid-600s and left written accounts of their doctrine. Only in more recent times have names of people earlier than Jesus become known more widely, such as Confucius or the Buddha, about whom Europeans knew nothing before the Mongol Empire. Other names of people connected with Jesus came alongside his, such as his mother Mary and the apostle Thomas. As a second wave, the first person *not* connected with Jesus whose name was known from England to China was probably Muhammad, since Bede wrote slanderous polemics against him in the 700s, and Muslim ambassadors and merchants came to China from the Abbasid caliphate. As the third wave, the first person connected with *neither* Jesus *nor* Muhammad whose name was known from England to China was probably Genghis Khan.

Genghis (or, better, Chinggis) Khan was acclaimed ruler of all who dwell in felt tents (including Mongols and other steppe nomads) in 1206, though some opposition remained. He began the conquest of northern China and Central Asia before he died in 1227. His son and successor Ögödei (d. 1241) finished conquering northern China and moved on to attack the southern Song dynasty, while also sending armies to attack Iran and eastern Europe. It was this last invasion, in Hungary and Poland in 1241 and 1242, that attracted the attention of western Europeans, and their diplomatic correspondence with the Mongols lasted the length of the Mongol Empire and its successor khanates. Ögödei's reign was followed by a long interregnum during which his widow, Töregene Khatun, exercised power for almost five years until their controversial son Güyük (r. 1246–48) was acclaimed as the great khan (*qa'an*).[3] After his death,

3. The basic title for a Mongol ruler is *khan* or *qan*. A "great khan" is known as a *khaghan*, *khaqan*, or *qa'an*, depending on the system for spelling Mongolian words.

Güyük's widow Oghul Qaimish served as regent for longer than her husband had reigned, until a different branch of Genghis's growing family was able to seize power for themselves in 1251. Led by Genghis Khan's daughter-in-law Sorqaqtani Beki, the widow of Ögödei's younger brother Tolui, this faction enthroned her son Möngke (r. 1251–59), Güyük's first cousin. All subsequent great khans would be descended from Tolui and Sorqaqtani Beki. Rabban Sawma was born in the aftermath of Genghis's first Mongol invasions in northern China, while his student Rabban Mark (later known as Yahballaha III) would have been born in the 1240s, when the Mongol Empire was firmly established from China to Russia and Iran but showing the first signs of strained unity.

The great khan Möngke continued the invasions of southern China but entrusted the further conquest of the Middle East to his brother Hülegü. The latter conquered Baghdad in 1258, and his generals captured Damascus briefly in 1260, until a defeat by the Mamluk army from Egypt forced them to withdraw. But Möngke's death in 1259 led to the permanent division of the Mongol Empire, as his two other brothers, Qubilai and Ariq-böke, fought a civil war for the ability to claim the title *qa'an*. Qubilai defeated his brother and was recognized by their brother Hülegü in far-off Iran, but not by his cousins who ruled Russia and the western steppe (what became "the Golden Horde") or his cousins who ruled in Central Asia, including Ögödei's grandson Qaidu (d. 1301). Though Qubilai went on to complete the conquest of China by crushing the southern Song dynasty in 1279, the Mongol Empire had been divided into separate and often warring khanates. When Rabban Sawma and Rabban Mark set out from China for Jerusalem, they had to navigate the conflicts between the great khan Qubilai in China and the independent Mongol rulers (including Qaidu) in Central Asia.

Qubilai (d. 1294) lived and reigned a long time as the great khan in China, but Hülegü died much earlier, in 1265 (as did his chief wife, long remembered in the Middle East as the Christian queen Doquz Khatun). But Hülegü started a dynasty of rulers, known as Ilkhans

A painting of Hülegü and Doquz Khatun, in a manuscript of the history of Rashid al-Din.

(from *il* meaning "submission" + khan) who effectively ruled Iraq and Iran independently while still nominally recognizing the supremacy of Qubilai and his successors in China, at least most of the time. In the aftermath of the Mongol Civil War, Hülegü also inaugurated the foreign policy of seeking a military alliance with western European rulers (all known as "Franks" in Middle Eastern texts) against the Mamluk Empire in Egypt and Syria, while the Golden Horde to the north made an alliance with the Mamluks against their common enemy, the Ilkhanate of Hülegü and his successors.

Hülegü's son Abaqa (r. 1265–82) continued his father's military and diplomatic objectives, fighting with the Chaghatai Khanate in Central Asia, the Golden Horde, and the Mamluks in Syria, while sending ambassadors to the Franks in Europe. He briefly corresponded with Lord Edward of England (the future King Edward I) while the latter was crusading in Palestine in 1271. Edward's intervention could have been significant, but it was mismanaged, and for all the Europeans' enthusiasm for the idea of recapturing Jerusalem, it would be several more centuries before they managed to bring an army to the eastern Mediterranean coast again. It was during Abaqa's reign that Rabban Sawma and Rabban Mark arrived in the Middle East, and Rabban Mark was elevated to the patriarchate as *catholicos* Mar Yahballaha III.[4]

Abaqa was succeeded by his brother Tegüder (r. 1282–84), who had also adopted the name Ahmad when he became Muslim. Some people, then and now, expected the new ruler's Islamic religion to drastically reshape his policy, but scholars debate whether to characterize his diplomatic outreach to Egypt as conciliatory or the same old demand for submission in a new Islamic vocabulary.[5] While the biography of Rabban Sawma and Yahballaha III presents Ahmad Tegüder as an oppressor of Christians, it also indicates that he was a tool being manipulated by others (Christian as well as Muslim) to cause harm to the *catholicos*, and other Christian sources remember Tegüder's reign more positively.[6] In any event, Tegüder was deposed before any significant difference in policy could be realized, and he was replaced by his brother, Abaqa's son Arghun (r. 1284–91).

Arghun continued the diplomatic goals of his father and grandfather, sending multiple embassies to the Franks in what was probably the most intensive phase of Mongol-European diplomacy. When Pope Nicholas IV responded favorably, Arghun had one of his sons (Öljeitü, a future Ilkhan) baptized and given the additional name Nicholas, in order to secure the alliance. But European military assistance never arrived in the Middle East, since the popes were usually more interested in converting the Ilkhans to Roman Catholic Christianity than in providing material support to a Mongol invasion of Syria, and the European kings preferred to maintain their own local quarrels. Arghun never invaded Syria himself,

4. The Church of the East used the titles *catholicos* and patriarch interchangeably for the leader of their denomination.

5. Judith Pfeiffer, "Aḥmad Tegüder's Second Letter to Qalā'ūn (682/1283)," in Judith Pfeiffer and Sholeh A. Quinn, eds., *History and Historiography of Post-Mongol Central Asia and the Middle East: Studies in Honor of John E. Woods* (Wiesbaden: Harrassowitz, 2006), 167–202.

6. Pier Giorgio Borbone, *The History of Mar Yahballaha and Rabban Sauma*, trans. Laura E. Parodi (Hamburg: Tredition Verlag, 2021), 344–45.

and the armies of Mamluk Egypt captured the last crusader stronghold on the Syrian coast at Acre between Arghun's death and the selection of a new Ilkhan. Arghun's brother and successor Geikhatu (r. 1291–95) is remembered primarily for his abundant generosity and disastrous economic policy: he attempted to introduce and enforce Chinese-style paper money in his capital city, Tabriz, leading to a complete shuttering of all legal commerce until he relented. When Geikhatu was killed in a rebellion in spring 1295, he was succeeded initially by a first cousin named Baidu, another grandson of Hülegü, and then by Arghun's son Ghazan, who came from his position as governor of Khorasan (northeastern Iran) to seize the throne from Baidu.

Ghazan's reign (1295–1304) is remembered as the greatest height of the Ilkhanate's power and glory, due in no small part to modern scholars' incomparable debt to Ghazan's vizier, historian, and propagandist, Rashid al-Din Hamadani (d. 1318), who is also mentioned in the biography of Rabban Sawma and Yahballaha III. Rashid al-Din took great pains to present his ruler and patron in the most glowing terms available to him, depicting Ghazan as a pious Muslim and a reformer of both Geikhatu's corruption and the pagan ways of the Mongols. Yet Ghazan's foreign policy closely resembled that of his predecessors, as he continued to seek a Frankish alliance against Mamluk Egypt. Unlike his father Arghun and his uncle Geikhatu, Ghazan invaded Syria no fewer than three times, achieving battlefield success but never managing to secure territorial gains. Ghazan's reign began with a turbulent period within the Ilkhanate, as he sought to root out the remaining supporters of his rival Baidu, and Christian sources recall the first eighteen months of his reign as a period of persecution, in which churches were confiscated and people were forced to convert to Islam. This period of violence is blamed in this source on Ghazan's supporter, the emir Nawruz, who was also Muslim and had earlier rebelled against Ghazan when the future Ilkhan was still governor of Khorasan. When Nawruz fell from the ruler's grace in 1297, he was hunted down and executed. The remainder of Ghazan's reign might well have seemed like a wonderful respite to both Christians and Muslims after the upheavals of the previous several years. Ghazan died at the age of thirty-two in 1304, with no sons, and was buried in a monumental mausoleum he had constructed outside of the capital city of Tabriz.

The Mongol nobles respected his wishes to enthrone his younger brother Öljeitü, then only twenty-two years old, after him. Though he had earlier been baptized, in service of his father Arghun's diplomacy with western Europe, by 1304 Öljeitü had become Muslim. He reportedly sponsored religious debates at his court between Muslims and non-Muslims, and even between Sunnis and Shiites. During his reign, peace was concluded among the four Mongol khanates that had fractured after the Mongol Civil War of the 1260s, a fact that Öljeitü announced in a letter to the king of France, and the Ilkhan continued seeking a western European alliance against the Mamluks in Egypt. Öljeitü invaded Syria again in 1312, but less effectively even than Ghazan's temporary successes. He constructed a new capital city at Sultaniyya, as well as a monumental mausoleum there that is still standing.

Öljeitü died in 1316 at the age of thirty-four and was succeeded officially by his young son Abu Saʿid (r. 1317–35), then only twelve years old. Various Mongol commanders gained power and competed for influence due to the Ilkhan's youth, but especially the "emir of emirs" ("commander of commanders") Chupan. Factionalism weakened the Ilkhanate, and Chupan stayed busy putting down rebellions of various emirs and defeating invasions from the Golden Horde and the Chaghatai Khanate, until Chupan himself rebelled against Abu Saʿid but was defeated in 1327. Abu Saʿid (and Chupan) had already signed a treaty ending the Ilkhanate's long-running war with Mamluk Egypt in 1322, which simultaneously ended the Ilkhan's search for an alliance with the fractious rulers of western Europe. European merchants and missionaries continued to pass through on occasion, and as late as the death of Timur Lenk (1405), some European powers held out hope of a "Mongol alliance" against "the Muslims" (though most western Mongols were now Muslim as well), yet no alliance ever materialized. When Abu Saʿid himself died in 1335 at thirty years old, he had no sons, brothers, or even first cousins. Other than his sister Sati Beg, who had been married to Chupan and was briefly acclaimed as the reigning queen (as a puppet in the power of Chupan's family), Abu Saʿid's closest relative was an elderly second cousin, the grandson of Geikhatu, whose father had been executed by Öljeitü. There was thus no consensus candidate for the throne of the Ilkhanate, and the rival factions of the Chupanid and Jalayirid clans put forward various nominal rulers as puppets under their respective control, but none of them achieved real power or widely recognized legitimacy. The Chupanid clan was eliminated by the Golden Horde in the 1350s, while the Jalayirids declared their independence and ruled from Baghdad, and other parts of the Ilkhans' vast lands were taken over by other new dynasties. The Mongol moment was over.

The Church of the East

Though many of us forget it now, Christianity was never only a Western religion. Christianity spread eastward across Asia just as rapidly as it spread westward across Europe. Whether or not the tradition of the apostle Thomas preaching in India is correct, Christians in Mesopotamia were sufficiently numerous to attract opposition from state-sponsored Zoroastrianism by 275, to have a metropolitan (an archbishop) residing in the Central Asian trading capital of Merv (Marw) in what is now Turkmenistan before 410, and for Christianity to be preached in China with the emperor's permission by 638, within a generation or two of Augustine of Canterbury being sent to England. Western European Christianity from an early period translated Greek into Latin, while the Christianity of Iraq and farther east used Syriac, a dialect of the widely distributed Aramaic language (of which Jesus himself spoke a different dialect). Syriac is identified as the variety of Aramaic spoken in Edessa, a Hellenistic cultural capital in northern Mesopotamia. Just as Western tradition ascribed the founding of their church to Peter and Paul in Rome, the tradition of the Syriac churches maintained the story that Christianity came to them through the apostle Thomas, his disciple Addai who went to Edessa, and Addai's disciple Mari (not Mary), who founded a church in Kokhe, one of the close cluster of cities that included Ctesiphon, the capital of the Sasanian Persian dynasty (224–651 CE) in southern Iraq. The "Liturgy of the Apostles" attributed to Addai and Mari continues to be celebrated in this denomination today, and the church (or throne) of Mar Mari in Kokhe continued to be necessary for enthroning new patriarchs of this denomination even after they moved their residence to Baghdad (founded as an Islamic capital in 762) and later Maragha (in northwestern Iran, which became a capital city of the Mongols).

Like other branches of Christianity, the Church of the East divided Christians into various categories, including clergy, monks (who might also be clergy) or nuns, and laypeople, the largest category, who were neither clergy nor monks or nuns.[7] The most common clergy were priests and deacons, found in every church, and some additional ranks of lower clergy were created, such as subdeacons and readers, each with their role to play in church services. As in every branch of Christianity other than the western European one, priests and deacons could be married and raise families.

Alongside the clergy, and overlapping with them, were the monks (and sometimes nuns). Syriac tradition reports that the practice of monks living together (cenobitic monasticism) was transplanted from Egypt to Syria by Mar Awgen in the 300s CE, though the actual origins of monasticism seem to be rather messier. Regardless of the movement's origins, in the medieval period monks were recognized by having a special haircut (a "tonsure"), wearing a special outfit (a "habit"), withdrawing from normal society, refusing to marry (celibacy), and refusing to acquire wealth (poverty). Most monks lived in monasteries with other monks, where they would live in a "cell" (Greek *kellos*, Syriac *qlītā*), but some monks lived alone as "recluses" either out in an uninhabited area or locked within their cell in the monastery and never leaving. Wilder varieties of monks such as anchorites (who moved from place to place without settling permanently) or stylites (who lived on the top of pillars) were occasionally observed. By their prayers, monks were thought to be powerful spiritual intercessors with God, for the guidance and protection of Christians. But

7. It is important to recognize, though scholars have generally failed to do so, that William of Rubruck's claim that all males were ordained priests even while still babies in the cradle is baseless slander intended to delegitimize his ecclesiastical rivals, not sober ethnographic reporting.

their decision to opt out of carrying on the family name and lineage also made the monks' way of life controversial with their parents.

Monks could be priests, but most were not, and priests could be monks, but most were not. But above the priests in the church hierarchy were the upper clergy, who all had to be monks as well. Bishops had responsibility primarily for a city and its surrounding region, although by the Mongol period there were also bishops appointed for nomadic groups and large areas with many cities in East Asia. A special kind of bishop, with bishops under his authority, was the metropolitan, corresponding partly to an archbishop and partly to a cardinal in western European Christianity. Above the metropolitans, at the apex of the hierarchy of the Church of the East, was the *catholicos*, the patriarch who functioned for Eastern Syriac Christians as the pope functioned for Western (Latin) Christians. The *catholicos* could also appoint special agents to represent him in places to which he was unable to travel; these representatives were sometimes called *chorepiscopoi* (from Greek), *periodeutai* (also from Greek), or "overseers" (Syriac *sāʿōrē*, singular *sāʿōrā*), and they roughly correspond to papal legates in western Europe. This could be a temporary appointment or a permanent one, and this was the office to which Rabban Sawma was appointed as "general overseer" (*sāʿōrā gāwānāyā*) when Yahballaha became *catholicos*. When a *catholicos* died, a nearby bishop administered the patriarchal household, while the metropolitan of Elam (in southeastern Iran) convened the nearby metropolitans in order to elect a successor. As the biography translated here makes plain, the clergy and laypeople of the city of Baghdad also participated in the deliberations.

The "cells" of *catholicos* patriarchs and of metropolitans were more than a single bedroom inhabited by the church leader alone, and therefore the many occurrences of "cell" in this biography, when referring to the residence of a high-ranking cleric, have been translated instead as "residence," often clarified as the patriarchal or metropolitan's residence when that is implicit in the Syriac text. The day-to-day operations of the "patriarchal cell" were managed by one or more "deacons" (who could also be priests or even a bishop), and many other people might live in the "patriarchal cell" at any given time. Metropolitans and bishops who visited him would stay in the "patriarchal cell," and there were often "disciples" who could run errands for the *catholicos* and serve practical functions, while being trained as monks and perhaps for future roles as bishops. A *catholicos* or metropolitan was also supposed to be generous to orphans, and often collected small children without families to live with him, some of whom became "disciples of the patriarchal cell." Some such members of the entourage of a *catholicos* should be presumed to be always present, and Yahballaha's biography makes more frequent mention of the younger occupants of the patriarchal residence than other medieval texts typically do.

Some readers will want to know what makes the Church of the East "different" from "normal" Christianity, but such a question of course presumes that western Christianity is "normal," a point the Church of the East today would likely dispute. Most differences would have been cultural, as the Church of the East developed in Iraq and farther east, in cultural contexts far removed from the late Roman Empire and the warrior culture that slowly replaced it, and direct contact between the easternmost and westernmost edges of Christianity was exceedingly rare before the Mongol period. Finicky theologians may wish to label the Church of the East "Nestorian" due to their failure to condemn the "errors" of Patriarch Nestorius of Constantinople (deposed 431), and indeed the Church of the East considered Nestorius to be a saint, though not a very important one for their theological tradition. After the (western) Council of Chalcedon in 451 redefined Aristotelian philosophical jargon in order to say that there are two "natures" but only one hypostasis in the incarnate Christ, Syriac Christians maintained the older Aristotelian usage but disagreed how it applied to Jesus: Western Syriac Christian leaders (polemically labeled "Jacobites," today called Syriac Orthodox) asserted that there was only one hypostasis (Syriac *qnōmā*) and *therefore* only one nature of God incarnate, while the Eastern Syriac Christian leaders (the Church of the East) insisted that Jesus has two natures, one divine and one human, unified permanently, and therefore two hypostases (Syriac *qnōmē*), but only one person (Greek *prosōpon*, Syriac *parṣōpā*) in Christ. The Armenian churches eventually (mostly) came to agree with the Western Syriac formulation. Such muddy depths of theology were rarely relevant for the function of the churches, except for identifying their relationships with other Christians who followed rival bishops. In the biography, such precise theological distinctions occur only in the section titled "Rabban Sawma's Creed, Which the Cardinals Requested from Him," and curiously the learned cardinals failed to recognize Rabban Sawma's expression of what they would have considered the heresy of Nestorianism. Instead they preferred to examine him regarding their fashionable theological controversy of the day, whether the Holy Spirit proceeds from the Father alone (the usual Greek position), from the Son alone (a bizarre position invented by these cardinals as a test for Rabban Sawma), or from both (the relatively new official position of the Roman papacy). As modern scholars are increasingly realizing, such theological niceties have loomed larger in the obsessions of theological pedants than in the practical experience of most Christians.[8]

The Church of the East is the only one of the ancient branches of Christianity never to have been a state-sponsored religion, though it did benefit from nonexclusive royal patronage from Sasanian *shahanshahs*,[9] Islamic caliphs and sultans, and Mongol Ilkhans. Farther east, away from Muslim rulers, Christianity spread among the nomads of the Eurasian steppe. The Kereyid (or Kerait) tribe was known to be largely Christian, from which tribe came Genghis Khan's first protector (named Toghril), as well as the mother of Hülegü and Qubilai and their brothers (Sorqaqtani Beki), Hülegü's queen (Doquz Khatun), and many others highly placed in Mongol society. The Önggüd Turkic tribe, into which Rabban Mark was born and perhaps Rabban Sawma likewise, was also known to contain many Christians. While Christianity experienced setbacks in China itself during the chaos following the fall of the Tang dynasty, it again flourished in China following the Mongol conquests and with the patronage of the great khans. When the cardinals in Rome expressed surprise that Christianity was found so far to the east, Rabban Sawma gently chided them for their ignorance of the wider world.

8. Jack B. V. Tannous, *The Making of the Medieval Middle East: Religion, Society, and Simple Believers* (Princeton, N.J.: Princeton University Press, 2020).

9. The Persian emperor's title *shahanshah* means "king of kings."

Christian-Muslim Relations

From its origins to the present day, Islam has existed in contact with other religions, and perhaps none of them more intensively than Christianity. Yet the interactions between Christians and Muslims are often misunderstood today, due to overly general attempts to characterize these interactions as either unceasing conflict (a "clash of civilizations") or generally harmonious coexistence (often termed *convivencia*). These two frameworks do more to advance modern political agendas than to improve our understanding of the intertwined history of the two largest world religions. One can find as many examples of violence or peacefulness as desired, but the reality was much more complicated than either characterization admits.

While westerners today often think "Christianity" refers first to medieval European Christendom, medieval Muslims in the Middle East often thought of "Christians" much closer at hand than faraway Europe. There was almost no religious segregation in the medieval Middle East, and under the powerful Abbasid caliphs of 700s and 800s CE, Christians often served as government bureaucrats and royal physicians. When Muslims employing non-Muslims became controversial, the caliph al-Mutawakkil (d. 861) issued an edict prohibiting everyone *other than the caliph* from hiring Christians. The prohibition did not work. Most of Greek medicine and philosophy were translated into Arabic in this period by Christian (and some Jewish) translators, and it is through these translations that Aristotle was eventually reintroduced to western European thinkers such as Thomas Aquinas. At the same time that the caliphs were waging wars against the Byzantine Empire, they were presiding over a multireligious court in Baghdad. As the empire of the Abbasid caliphs waned and fragmented after 900 CE, and especially as the (Muslim) Seljuk Turks conquered most of the caliphate and much of the Byzantine Empire after 1050 CE, previously customary ways of Christians and Muslims interacting needed to be renegotiated with new rulers, often on a more local geographical scale.

Under Muslim rulers, various theories were proposed of the proper relationships between Muslims and Christians in society. The most tenacious of these was the collection of *jizya*, a discriminatory tax on non-Muslim individuals that was regarded as humiliating, and was mandated in the Qur'an, the Islamic holy book. A separate set of ideas, independent of the Qur'an, included the wearing of distinctive clothing (Arabic *ghiyār*), which for Christians in the period shortly before the Mongol invasions usually took the form of a wide belt (Arabic *zunnār*, from Greek *zōnarion*). In reality, enforcement of clothing differentiation and other measures was often haphazard and inconsistent throughout the medieval era. While the conquests of the pagan Mongols swept away these ideas for a time, as the Mongols converted to Islam, their (non-Mongol) Muslim advisors increasingly advocated for the restoration of such discriminatory policies and a return to the government-recognized supremacy of Islam over other religions as practiced by pre-Mongol rulers.

But the Christians under Mongol rule sometimes had other ideas. The actual process by which the *jizya* and the wide belt were reenacted and enforced in practice continued to be inconsistent until the end of the Ilkhanate, but they were sometimes required and much loathed by the Christians subject to them. When Ghazan came to the throne, Christians were again required to pay the *jizya* and wear wide belts, but then the requirements were abolished again after his chief supporter emir Nawruz fell from favor. The *jizya* and differential clothing requirements were reinstated under Öljeitü, but then temporarily lifted again after appeals from multiple Christian leaders. More dramatically, these conflicting Christian and Muslim ideas about the relationship between Mongol imperial rule and religious hierarchy provide the background to the two sieges of Christians in Arbil mentioned in this primary source. The Mongol armies included non-Mongol units, among which were groups of soldiers trained to fight in the mountains (here called *qāyājīs*), unlike the Mongols themselves who fought best in open grasslands. Many if not all of these "mountaineers" were recruited from Christian populations (Georgian, Armenian, Syriac) in the highlands between what is today eastern Turkey and northwestern Iran, and as loyal fighters in the service of the Mongol khans, they no doubt felt superior to civilians, even Muslim civilians, in the cities of the Ilkhanate. In 1297 and again in

1310, trouble arose between these *qāyājīs* and Muslims in Arbil, a city in what is today Iraqi Kurdistan.

In 1297, after eighteen months of persecution of Christians that the author of this text blames on the Muslim Mongol emir Nawruz, the Mongol ruler Ghazan decided to arrest and execute this supporter who had helped put him on the throne in 1295, but the task turned out to be more difficult than anticipated and took six months of hunting to capture the fugitive. During the same spring and summer, according to this text, Muslims in the city of Arbil decided to destroy a Christian church located in the city's well-fortified citadel, a fortress large enough to contain not only soldiers but also a civilian residential population. But the church was defended by the Christian *qāyājīs*, in the process of which they shot at and killed "a famous man" (unidentified, but perhaps a Mongol). This was interpreted not only by the Muslims but also by the local Mongol garrison as an act of rebellion against the Ilkhanate, and the forces outside laid siege to the Christians in the citadel. The people besieged in the citadel faced the difficulty of not being able to present their explanation of the conflict at court, so the ruler heard only the viewpoint of their enemies. It took the capture and execution of Nawruz, careful rhetoric and extensive negotiations by Yahballaha III, and large sums of money to accomplish a settlement of the crisis. In a frankly surprising show of mercy, which the author attributes to divine intervention, Ghazan allowed the Christians to remain in the citadel, creating a situation in which the population of Arbil was partially religiously segregated, with most people in the lower city Muslim and most people in the citadel Christian.

Thirteen years later, a similar crisis in the same location ended much more violently, the story of which occupies a large portion of the end of this narrative. Unlike the earlier crisis after the upheavals of Ghazan's early reign, in 1310 Öljeitü's reign was secure, but Yahballaha III now had less influence on the Mongol court. In recent years he had spent more time away from the royal encampment, as he was getting older and finding constant travel more taxing. The author also blames Öljeitü's Islam for this loss of influence (implausibly, since Ghazan was likewise Muslim) by claiming that Öljeitü did not summon

Yahballaha to court like his predecessor had. Nevertheless, the author does concede that when Yahballaha III visited the royal encampment, he was honored by the Mongol ruler, though allegedly "not from the heart." The author also engages in conspiratorial thinking, choosing to believe that all Muslims were longing to destroy the Christian community in the Arbil citadel, as they had allegedly attempted and failed to accomplish in 1297, despite the fact that his own account includes several Muslim Mongols (such as Chupan) who tried to help the besieged Christians in the citadel. The author (who was likely in Arbil at the start of the crisis, if the hypothesis of his identity is correct) also blames the restive Christian "mountaineers" (*qāyājīs*) stationed in the citadel for infighting and complaining against their commander, which prompted Öljeitü to replace him with Nasir Dilqandi, a Muslim commander and the person who prompted the crisis. Finally, the author sees in the catastrophe divine judgment on the sins of the Christians living in the Arbil citadel.

Conflict between the *qāyājīs* and the new commander Nasir Dilqandi led him to label them rebels, which was confirmed when the Christian *qāyājīs* resisted a command from Öljeitü to leave the citadel of Arbil in March 1310. The author faults the Christians and even Yahballaha III himself for failing to go to the royal encampment to explain the situation, which might have averted the catastrophe. Attempts to reach a negotiated settlement, such as ended the earlier crisis in 1297, nearly succeeded in resolving the situation in late April, in mid-May, and again in late June, but ultimately the Ilkhans' commands to end the siege without harm to the besieged Christians of the citadel failed to prevent a massacre, and the citadel was taken back under Mongol control at the beginning of July 1310. Empires then as now regarded any perceived rebellion as requiring a serious response, and while the author of this primary source presents the conflict as one between Christians and Muslims, it is clear that the Mongol commanders and rulers viewed the issue as rebellion by the inhabitants of the Arbil citadel against Mongol rule itself. That those rebellious inhabitants were Christian was considered irrelevant by some Mongols, and by others, as further proof of their disloyalty.

Rabban Sawma and Mar Yahballaha III

In the context of the Mongol Empire of Genghis Khan, the Church of the East, and the long trajectory of relations between Christians and Muslims, two men born in what is today China crossed the width of Asia and played a key role in politics and religion in the Middle East. The joint biography translated here is not the only primary source for their lives, since they were noticed by their contemporaries. A short overview of their lives, as known from this and other texts, might help prepare readers to understand the biography that was produced.

The older of the two was named Sawma, a name that means "fasting" or refers to the church season of Lent, preceding Easter. He was born near what became Beijing, though at the time he was born, that capital city had not yet been founded by the Mongols. The biography refers to Sawma and his younger follower as "eastern Turks," while other sources label them "Uyghurs"; it is likely that Middle Eastern sources were not extraordinarily precise in distinguishing ethnicities in East Asia. But he was the only child of older parents, conceived with difficulty (unless that is a trope) and raised as a Christian, who withdrew from the normal expectations of marrying and carrying on the family line in order to become a hermit monk. His fame as a Christian holy man seems to have attracted a follower named Mark, born around 1244 to a family in the city of Kosheng, in the region inhabited by the Önggüd Turks, and the two of them decided to set out on a pilgrimage to Jerusalem around 1275. Some sources, though not all, say that the pair were in fact commanded to travel to Jerusalem on behalf of Qubilai, the great khan (*qa'an*), a detail omitted in this biography. The journey for the two monks across Central Asia took them across war zones and was more difficult than either expected, so that entering a monastery in northeastern Iran felt like being reborn.

These two pilgrims reached Iraq, but there was no available route onward to Jerusalem, due to ongoing warfare between the Mongol Ilkhans, who ruled Iran and Iraq, and the Mamluk Empire, which ruled Egypt and Syria, including Jerusalem. Forced to abandon their pilgrimage, they lived in monasteries in Iraq and caught the attention of the *catholicos* of the time, Denha, who recognized the value of having church leaders who understood the Mongols' language and customs. He involved them in his relationships with the Ilkhan Abaqa (d. 1282) and ultimately decided to send them back to East Asia to be regional leaders of their Christian denomination. Thus in 1279 he ordained Rabban Mark as the metropolitan of Ong and Katai (i.e., the Önggüd lands and northern China), with the new name Mar Yahballaha, and the *catholicos* ordained Rabban Sawma as a "general overseer" to assist the new metropolitan. Yet by that time, the path back across Central Asia was unsafe, due to warfare between the Ilkhanate and the Chaghatai Khanate, so the two travelers continued to be stuck in Iraq. After the *catholicos* Denha died in 1281, the metropolitans of the Church of the East met in Baghdad and chose Yahballaha to be his replacement, explicitly due to his familiarity with the Mongols, and he was confirmed as the new *catholicos* by Abaqa, who granted him an annual stipend. When Abaqa died in 1282, he was succeeded as Ilkhan by his son Tegüder (known as Ahmad in the biography translated here), who was a Muslim. Tegüder's relationship with Yahballaha III was initially more strained, and the annual stipend was discontinued. The author of the biography blames Tegüder's Islam for the tension but also indicates the roles played by ambitious Christian leaders who sought to get Yahballaha deposed, as well as Muslim government officials. By contrast, other Christian texts from the time remember Tegüder more favorably. In any event, Tegüder was ousted in 1284 by the rebellion of his brother Arghun.

Under Arghun, Rabban Sawma reached the pinnacle of his fame. In pursuit of an alliance with European crusaders against their common enemy, the Mamluk Empire in Egypt and Syria, Arghun sent a series of diplomatic missions to the Franks in western Europe. Rabban Sawma was sent as an ambassador in 1287, only to discover that the pope had died earlier that year, which prevented him from completing his mission until a new pope was elected in early 1288. After visiting the kings of France and England (the former in Paris, the latter located in southern France),[10] Rabban Sawma spent the winter in Genoa, the home of

10. The Plantagenet dynasty which ruled England at the time also governed the duchy of Aquitaine in southwestern France under the sovereignty of the French monarchy.

one of his fellow ambassadors, until he received word of the election of Pope Nicholas IV, to whom he delivered the letters, messages, and gifts from Arghun and Yahballaha. They stayed in Rome through Easter of that year, then returned to Arghun in Tabriz, carrying gifts and letters from the pope and the European kings. As part of this diplomacy, after Rabban Sawma returned, Arghun commanded Yahballaha III to baptize the Ilkhan's young son Öljeitü, giving him the additional name Nicholas, in honor of the new pope. Yahballaha III continued to correspond with later popes, of which two of his letters to Boniface VIII survive.

In addition to this diplomatic activity, Yahballaha III and Rabban Sawma were involved in building churches and monasteries. Yahballaha renovated and enlarged a church in Maragha early in Arghun's reign, and when Rabban Sawma returned from Europe, Arghun endowed a tent church within the Mongol royal encampment, which moved with the rest of the royal household. After Arghun's death, during the reign of his famously generous brother Geikhatu (r. 1291–95), Rabban Sawma retired from the annual nomadic movement of the royal camp and built another church in Maragha. Rabban Sawma passed away in Baghdad on January 10, 1294, and was buried in the "Court of the Romans," the residence of the earlier *catholicos* patriarchs of the Church of the East. Later that year, Yahballaha began building a monastery just outside Maragha.

When Geikhatu was killed in early 1295, a more difficult period developed for Yahballaha, as Geikhatu was briefly succeeded by his cousin Baidu, who favored Christians, but by September Baidu himself was defeated and executed by Arghun's son Ghazan, who was Muslim and had been put on the throne by a Muslim Mongol emir named Nawruz. Various sources report confiscations of church buildings and violence against Christians (and, incidentally, Buddhists) in cities across the Ilkhanate during the first eighteen months of Ghazan's reign, as the new ruler consolidated his power and the loyalties of Christians were suspected to favor his defeated rival Baidu. Yahballaha faced repeated violence and extortion from various individuals and groups during this time, with occasional respites when he was able to claim protection from more powerful patrons. But after Nawruz fell from Ghazan's grace in 1297,

Yahballaha received more consistent honor and gifts from the Ilkhan, allowing him to rebuild his earlier church and monastery at Maragha. It is during Ghazan's reign that Yahballaha seems to be most consistently traveling with the royal camp, even celebrating the Mongol New Year in the city of al-Hilla in southern Iraq.

After Ghazan died in 1304, he was succeeded by his brother Öljeitü, who had become a Muslim in the years since he had been baptized by Yahballaha III. The *catholicos* seems to have had a more distant relationship with the royal encampment after 1304, as he established a new patriarchal residence ("cell") in the citadel of the city of Arbil in northern Iraq and spent increasing amounts of time there. Thus he was in the citadel itself at the outbreak of the crisis of 1310, and he participated in various attempts to resolve the crisis peacefully. He spent much of that period as a prisoner of the Mongol commander in charge of ending the standoff (one way or another), part of the time locked into the citadel itself, and part of it in a village nearby. In any event he watched in horror as the situation went from bad to worse, and he was unable to effectually rescue the Christians of the city. Following that disaster, he again went to the royal camp and received honor from Öljeitü and other members of the Mongol royal family, but afterward he reportedly withdrew to the monastery outside Maragha that he had built, where he died on November 15, 1317.

The Author and Composition of the Text

The author is not named in the manuscripts and does not identify himself in the text, so our knowledge of the author is in the first instance based on clues within the text. The author begins his biography of these two church leaders by an extensive theological meditation on divine providence, and he was so familiar with the variable hymns of the church services that he often gives the date of events not according to the month and day of the calendar, but according to the Sunday on which a particular hymn is to be chanted in the liturgy. He indicates that Rabban

Sawma's own travel account contained much more than he translated into Syriac, but the notes from that journey included in his text focus primarily on relics, church architecture, and the papal liturgies of the Easter season in Rome. When the siege of the Christians in the citadel of Arbil ends disastrously, the author laments in words taken directly from the biblical book of Lamentations, rephrased to refer to "the church." With the ability to compose in Syriac and at least to read Persian (to be able to translate Rabban Sawma's travelogue), the author clearly was a priest or other church leader in the denomination of Yahballaha III and Rabban Sawma, the Church of the East.

Beyond that is guesswork, but guesses can sometimes be confirmed by reexamining the evidence. Heleen Murre-van den Berg first proposed that the unnamed author was none other than Mar Yahballaha's successor as *catholicos*, Timothy II.[11] She observed that the metropolitan of Arbil during the 1310 siege plays a large role in the narrative but is the only significant figure in the text who is not named, and we know from another source that Timothy II had been the metropolitan of Arbil, named Joseph, before his election as *catholicos*.[12] Murre-van den Berg proposes that the extensive discussion of the metropolitan's ultimately thwarted attempts to rescue the Christians of Arbil make this text a defense of that church leader against criticism.[13] I would add that not only is the metropolitan of Arbil the only major character not named, his name is deliberately suppressed: he is once referred to by Yahballaha as "Metropolitan *so-and-so* of this place."[14] This is the only use of "so-and-so" (Syriac *plān*) in the whole text; other minor characters

11. Heleen Murre-van den Berg, "The Church of the East in Mesopotamia in the Mongol Period," in Roman Malek with Peter Hofrichter, eds., *Jingjiao: The Church of the East in China and Central Asia* (Sankt Augustin: Institut Monumenta Serica, 2006), 391–93.

12. Herman G. B. Teule, "The Synod of Timotheos II—1318," in Alberto Melloni and Ephrem Ishac, eds., *The General Councils of the Eastern Christian Churches* (Turnhout, Belgium: Brepols, 2023), 2:1455.

13. Murre-van den Berg, "The Church of the East in Mesopotamia," 392.

14. See p. 133 of the translation. Italics added for emphasis.

are simply unnamed. Obviously Yahballaha III knew the metropolitan's name, and given the author's extensive reporting of the event and naming every other major participant, he must have known as well. But in the Syriac literary tradition, it was considered boasting to write one's own name in one's book, and suppressing one's name was a mark of humility appropriate for a monk or church leader. Further, this metropolitan of Arbil is the only person other than Yahballaha whose interior thoughts are reported in the narrative. While it may be impossible to prove conclusively that Timothy II, the former metropolitan of Arbil, is the author of this biography, it seems by far the most plausible explanation of these odd features of the text.

Not much else is known about Timothy II, however. He had been bishop of Mosul before he became metropolitan of Arbil, though it is unknown when he assumed either office. He was elected *catholicos* of the Church of the East in 1318, but the date of his death is as unknown as the date of his birth. Based on dating formulas in surviving manuscripts, he seems to have been still in office in 1328, but his successor Denha II was consecrated as the *catholicos* in 1336, so he must have died before then. Of Timothy II's acts in office, all that is known is that upon becoming *catholicos* he held a council to reform the church, whose decisions are recorded, and at some point he composed a commentary on the seven sacraments in Syriac. The text of this story mentions that the metropolitan of Arbil had a younger brother, but nothing else is known about him.

The biography contains evidence that it was composed over a long period of time. Of course Rabban Sawma composed his travel account in Persian during or immediately after his return from western Europe in 1288, and the abridged Syriac translation of Rabban Sawma's account, which is included in this text, occasionally preserves a "we" from the Persian source, which does not reflect the author of the Syriac biography. Yet when the Syriac text describes Rabban Sawma's church, it says, "To this day he is its glory, and prayers and offerings are continual in it," which may suggest that this description was first penned before Rabban Sawma's death in 1294, though perhaps this means merely that the glory of that particular church is having had such an eminent founder. More concrete evidence is the use of parenthetical benedictions, asking for the Ilkhan Ghazan (d. 1304), the emir Irinjin (d. 1319), and the emir of emirs Chupan (d. 1327) to be "preserved in life," which suggests that the text was already being composed during the lifetime of Ghazan (before 1304), even though it continued being composed until after the death of Mar Yahballaha in 1317. Given that the composition of the text spread over at least a couple decades, the place of its composition probably similarly varied, but as Heleen Murre-van den Berg observed, after Rabban Sawma's return from Europe the horizons of the text constrict to Iraq and northwestern Iran, with special focus on Arbil. The text was probably composed partly in northern Iraq and partly in northwestern Iran.

The text fits uneasily within a few different genres. On one level, it is a joint biography of two special monks who rise to positions of leadership within the church hierarchy, and the first portion of the text reads like many other saints' lives and hagiographical texts, complete with tropes of overcoming worldly obstacles in order to fulfill one's monastic vocation, and the devout desire to go on pilgrimage to Jerusalem. The beginning of their pilgrimage introduces another relevant genre, the travel account, which follows first their itinerary from China to the Middle East and then Rabban Sawma's travels to western Europe, providing some details about what they saw and whom they met along the way. Yet they never reached Jerusalem. Instead, hagiographic glorification gives way to a political biography of Yahballaha III under Mongol rule, tracing his shifting relationships with the successive Ilkhans governing Iran and Iraq, from Abaqa (d. 1282) until Öljeitü (d. 1316). But then more than a fifth of the text is dedicated to one episode, the siege of the Christians in the citadel of Arbil in 1310, an episode in which the *catholicos* plays a significant (and largely negative) role, but he is not always the center of the narrative action. Here the author shifts fully into the lament genre, mourning the destruction of his Christian community, including castigating the Christians for their sins and extensively echoing the biblical book of Lamentations. The last seven years of the *catholicos*'s life are reported tersely, as an afterthought. So the text is a biography, but one whose focus occasionally drifts and incorporates other genres.

The audience and purpose of the text need to be understood in light of its composition. As a text authored in Syriac, its primary audience would be those who could read such a language, which by the Mongol period would be primarily limited to clergy and their family members. In the early stages of the composition, during the reign of Ghazan, when Rabban Sawma and Yahballaha III had corresponded with popes and built elaborate churches and monasteries, the purpose of this narrative was undoubtedly to glorify the two protagonists as holy monks guided by God who led the church, and the *catholicos* in particular held on to the faith even while suffering tortures from his enemies in the early 1280s and again in 1295. Yet the narrator also criticizes Yahballaha's naivete at several points, especially during the 1310 siege of the citadel of Arbil, which suggests that the political biography can be read for its lessons on what to imitate and what not to imitate, even in the hero of the story. The account of the metropolitan's actions during that same siege serves to vindicate his attempts to rescue the situation, even though they were ultimately unsuccessful, and that portion of the text may serve as a defense for Yahballaha's successor. Ultimately, Yahballaha's conclusion, "I am tired of serving the Mongols," may serve as a warning to churchmen of the dangers of seeking too close a relationship with political power, especially as the Mongol rulers turned to Islam.[15]

These reflections on genre, audience, and purpose need to shape all assessment of the historical value of this source. Any text that covers from China in the 1220s to Europe in the 1280s to Iraq in the 1310s will necessarily be heterogeneous. The author's information about the family background and upbringing of Rabban Sawma and Mar Yahballaha was necessarily conveyed by the protagonists themselves, but then reworked in light of the conventions of saints' lives as a genre, such as parental opposition to children becoming monks. Rabban Sawma's diplomatic journey to Europe contains all the pitfalls and potential usefulness of travelogues: they report details that the locals might not have considered noteworthy (such as architectural and agricultural details), while also

15. If this interpretation is accurate, it may also explain the author's decision to omit any reference to Qubilai sending Rabban Sawma and Rabban Mark to Jerusalem, as that would tie their travel to worldly Mongol authority rather than to independent spiritual inspiration.

being unable to distinguish which of the things witnessed were typical and which were unusual. The long narrative of the siege of the citadel of Arbil highlights aspects that fit the author's lament, such as the sinfulness or neglect of the Christians, the demoniacal enmity he ascribes to the Muslims, and the justice of divine action in bringing this punishment upon them. In order to use this biography most profitably as the rich historical source that it is for politics, religion, and society across the width of Eurasia, it needs to be read critically.

Being Polite or Its Opposite

Being polite was essential in the medieval Middle East, and it shaped everything written in that period, in ways that defy translation into English. For example, when addressing someone politely it is important to highlight their high rank, virtue, splendor, power, and so forth, meaning that a common way of saying "you" was to say "your fatherhood" or "your holiness." English speakers still do this in fossilized phrases by addressing kings as "your majesty" and judges as "your honor," though perhaps surprisingly, in this biography speakers do not use this form of speech to address kings, preferring instead to say, "O king, live forever!" Conversely, when referring to oneself, it was important to emphasize one's lowliness, unworthiness, inability, servility, and so on; one way of saying "I" is by referring to "my weakness." My own inability to render these into clear English in a way that will immediately communicate the intent to the uninitiated has caused the following translation to replace most such polite phrases with "you" and "I," respectively.

Another feature of medieval Middle Eastern politeness was to address someone as "my lord" or "my lady," and to refer to oneself as "your servant." While fossilized traces of this again survive into modern English, in fact its usage in medieval Syriac exceeds anything comprehensible to the modern reader. Thus the honorific "Mar" that precedes Yahballaha's name is "my lord" in Syriac, and it occurs before every instance of his name in the text, including in the narrative. "Mar" (or the feminine "Mart") also precedes every name of every saint (where it has been replaced by the more usual English honorific "Saint"), as well as references to the Cross of Christ (*mār ṣlībā*, "my lord the Cross") and Zion as a poetic name for Jerusalem (*mār ṣehyōn*, "my lord Zion"), in ways for which there is no corresponding English custom (and so is sometimes translated "holy" or "revered" in the text that follows). "Mar" also precedes most, but not all, occurrences of the titles "*catholicos*" and "pope," but since this translator judged it off-putting for a narrator to be continually referencing "my lord the *catholicos*" or "my lord the pope," in third-person narration the phrase has been replaced with "the lord," though occasionally in reported speech it made sense to preserve "my lord" as a form of direct address.

Politeness also accounts for one of the trickiest portions of the text to read, namely, Rabban Sawma's encounter with the pope. Among the polemics and apologetics of modern Roman Catholics and Protestants, to accept the pope at all is to recognize his claims of authority over the entire church, but the situation looked rather different from medieval Baghdad or Maragha. The Church of the East had only very infrequent contact with the Roman papacy, as Rabban Sawma himself says to the cardinals on his first visit to Rome, yet they might be content to accept him as a brother patriarch, as they were sometimes willing to recognize the Patriarch of Constantinople. A tenth-century Eastern Syriac author named Emmanuel Bar Shahhare had proposed that five patriarchates were set up by the apostles, in Rome, Constantinople, Antioch, Alexandria, and Seleucia-Ctesiphon (the capital of the Sasanian Persian Empire), each with regional jurisdiction.

From such a perspective, the Church of the East simply was not confronted with papal claims for exclusive universal authority, either to accept or reject them. So when Rabban Sawma prays for the newly elected Pope Nicholas IV to be a blessing for the church, or for the papal throne to be established forever, this does not imply considering the pope his superior. Similarly, when the cardinals asked Rabban Sawma whether he believes what the pope believes or something else (making papal doctrine the touchstone of orthodoxy), he replied that he believes what the apostles taught but is uninformed about what the popes might believe. When Rabban Sawma asked for the pope's permission to depart or to celebrate his own liturgy, this does not imply subordination to papal authority but rather conformity to protocol as the Mongol ambassador and a foreign guest. There is no doubt that Pope Nicholas IV viewed his open letters to Mar Yahballaha and to Rabban Sawma as formally investing them in their offices, reflecting his claims of universal authority, but it seems equally certain that the author of this text presents the pope merely as the "*catholicos* patriarch of Romania [the land of the Romans] and of all the Westerners," on an equal footing with Yahballaha III, the "*catholicos* patriarch of the East."[16]

Yahballaha's letters to later popes, dated 1302 and 1304, have long been taken as evidence that he at least accepted papal supremacy, since they contain a key phrase asserting a duty of obedience to the papacy. But this phrase was in fact inserted into the Latin translation and does not occur in the Arabic original.[17] Yahballaha III wrote nothing about obeying the pope, and when he refers to the pope as Christ's "deputy" (Arabic *khalīfa*, from which we get the English word "caliph"), this does not invoke Latin understandings of the "Vicar of Christ," though the medieval translators chose to represent it that way.[18] The letters' references to the pope as the "father of fathers" were merely using the language of any patriarchate. Yahballaha III, like Rabban Sawma before him, was being very polite, and too many modern scholars have been misled by medieval Latin translators rather than consulting the Arabic originals.

The opposite of politeness is not rudeness but execration, the ability to call down curses on one's enemies, which has likewise shaped this biography. Thus people who cause trouble for the author's own community

16. See pp. 42 and 88 of the translation.

17. Dietmar W. Winkler, "Two Letters of Yahballaha III to the Popes of Rome: Historical Context and English Translation," in Li Tang and Dietmar W. Winkler, eds., *Artifact, Text, Context: Studies on Syriac Christianity in China and Central Asia* (Münster: LIT Verlag, 2020), 220–21.

18. Laura E. Bottini, "Due lettere inedite del patriarca mar Yahballaha III (1281–1317)," *Rivista degli studi orientali* (1992): 245.

(and especially the emir Nawruz) are referred to as "cursed" or similar phrases. Just as blessings might be inserted in parentheses after any mention of a king or favored patron, so curses might be inserted with each mention of an enemy to be execrated. The author's extremely negative characterization of "the Muslim people" partially partakes of this tradition, while also crossing into the realm of negative stereotyping. (Indeed, the author gives evidence to undermine his hostile depiction of "the Muslim people," as some Muslim civilians in Arbil sheltered Christians during the rioting, and the emir Chupan who intervened on behalf of the Christians was himself a Muslim who requested to be buried in Medina.) While the author presents an oversimplified negative stereotype of "the Muslim people" as always hating Christians, it is also important to recognize the place of the inverse of politeness in the culture of his time. In a sense, some extreme Christian and Muslim partisans at the time, including the author of this biography, were engaged in a "culture war" through which they viewed developments, and they sought to enlist their coreligionists on their side, while most Christians and Muslims at the time did not see relationships across the religious difference as necessarily hostile. For church leaders in particular, presenting Muslims as always hostile might also serve to discourage conversion to Islam among one's fellow Christians. Execration and negative stereotyping were (and are) techniques used by the extremists to force the more amiable bulk of the population to pick sides.

Keeping Time

The biography of Rabban Sawma and Yahballaha III covers almost a century, and it uses multiple ways of keeping time to indicate when events happened. Most surprisingly, it makes no reference to the Islamic lunar calendar, in which months correspond to the cycles of the moon and twelve new moons comprise a year. It also makes no reference to the Chinese zodiac, in which years are associated with one of twelve animals in a repeating cycle. It makes only one brief reference to Mongol methods of reckoning time, when it alludes to the "White Feast" of the Mongols, which is the "White Moon" of the Mongolian new year (corresponding to the Chinese new year, the second new moon after the winter solstice). There is similarly one reference to the ancient Babylonian zodiac, a reference to the sun moving into "the sign of Aries" in the spring.

Instead, the usual way of marking years was based on the Seleucid era, while two systems coexisted for marking time within a year, one based on the cycle of church services and the other on a cycle of months. The Seleucid era was known in medieval Syriac texts as "the year of the Greeks," though it did not in fact count years since the reign of Alexander the Great, as medieval authors believed. Instead it counted solar years that had passed since an event almost no one remembered, the entrance of one of Alexander's successors, Seleukos I Nikator, into Babylon in 312 BCE. (Seleukos later regarded that event as the founding of his empire, named the Seleucid Empire after him.) Each year is 365 days long, except for leap years (one year in every four), which are 366 days long. The "year of the Greeks" (AG for *anno graecorum*) began on October 1 each year, so from January 1 to September 30 one can convert from AG to CE by subtracting 311, and from October 1 to December 31 by subtracting 312.

Syriac Christians divided each year into twelve months, inheriting their names in many cases from Akkadian names used in ancient Babylon. But by the late medieval period, each month had developed a length corresponding to a month in the Julian calendar, so that First Teshri (31 days) always corresponded to October, Second Teshri (30 days) to November, First Kanon (31 days) to December, Second Kanon (31 days) to January, Shevat (28 or 29 days) to February, Adar (31 days) to March, Nisan (30 days) to April, Iyar (31 days) to May, Haziran (30 days) to June, Tammuz (31 days) to July, Ab (31 days) to August, and Ilol (30 days) to September. To facilitate reading, Syriac month names have been replaced by the corresponding English month's name in the translation.

But Syriac Christian clergy used another method for indicating dates within a year, one based on the church calendar and the changing shape of the church service throughout the year. Some church feasts occurred on fixed calendar dates, such as Christmas (*yaldā* or "Nativity" in Syriac) on

December 25 and the Feast of the Cross (*shkhāḥtā* or "Finding" in Syriac) on September 13. Other feasts, such as Easter (*qyāmtā* or "Resurrection" in Syriac), were originally tied to lunar cycles that shifted relative to the solar calendar's dates, and by the late medieval period the dates of such feasts were calculated using a complicated system that corresponded neither to solar nor lunar phenomena (eventually prompting the Gregorian calendar reform). The calculation of the Easter date for each year was an important part of marking time, since roughly half of each year was counted as leading up to Easter (starting three weeks before the beginning of Lent, with a fast known as the Petition of the Ninevites) or following from it (through Pentecost, considered the first Sunday of seven Sundays dedicated to the apostles). Each Sunday, whether counted from the beginning or end of the year or counted before or after Easter, had some hymns that were only to be sung on that Sunday, and by referring to "the Sunday of the hymn *aynāw āsyā*," for example, a clerical author could quickly identify for other priests when in the cycle of church services an event occurred. The hymn "titles" are always just the opening words of the hymn (as is usually the case in medieval Latin hymns as well), for which reason they have not been translated in the following text, but in each case the day and month have been calculated and supplied in brackets to assist the reader.

The Transmission of the Text

When this biography was completed in the aftermath of the death of Yahballaha III, it existed only in a single copy handwritten by either the author himself or a scribe to which he gave dictation. How was this biography preserved and transmitted, so that today it has been read across Eurasia and in the Americas?

The earliest stages of the transmission of the text are very unclear. As is commonly the case with the literature of the Church of the East, it must have been copied repeatedly in the centuries following its composition, but the earliest known manuscript today only comes from the 1880s.

Until that time, knowledge of the text does not seem to have extended beyond a small region in the Hakkari Mountains of what is today eastern Turkey. An elderly local monk named Rabban Yonan found a manuscript in a small village, made a copy of it, and sent it to the city of Urmia (now in northwestern Iran) in 1885 by the means of a priest named Oshaʿna, who showed it to American missionaries there. They announced the discovery of this biography to a western audience, but before they published the Syriac text, it was already printed in Europe in 1888 by a Lazarist Catholic priest named Paul Bedjan on the basis of a manuscript newly copied in Urmia in 1887. Four additional manuscript copies, all made in the 1880s, came to light in the next few years, prompting Bedjan to issue an improved edition of the Syriac text in 1895. Of these manuscripts, only three are accessible today.[19]

Translations soon followed, first into French by Jean-Baptiste Chabot (1895), English by James A. Montgomery (1927, partial) and Ernest A. W. Budge (1928), Russian by Nina Pigulevskaia (1958), Neo-Aramaic by Mattay d-Bet Petros (1961), German by Franz Altheim (1961, partial), Arabic by Louis Sako (1974, partial), Italian by Pier Giorgio Borbone (2000), German by Alexander Toepel (2008, complete), and French by Pier Giorgio Borbone and E. Alexandre (2008). In English, Montgomery's translation provides only the first part of the text, while Budge's translation, though complete, contains a number of misunderstandings due to his primary expertise being located in the Ancient Near East, where he extensively translated ancient Assyrian and Egyptian texts. For as long as I have been interested in medieval Syriac (and likely much longer), scholars have been complaining about the quality of Budge's translation and wishing for a replacement. Pier Giorgio Borbone and Laura Parodi provided the first complete English translation since Budge's in 2021.

Scholars who wish to use this text for research will still need to consult Pier Giorgio Borbone's Syriac edition and Laura Parodi's English translation published by Tredition, which includes Borbone's extensive commentary and textual notes. The translation presented here is revised

19. For details, see Borbone, *History of Mar Yahballaha*, 13–15, 58–71.

from that translation, chiefly with the aim of making it more accessible to North American undergraduates, including some who do not have the broad vocabulary displayed there. Some annotations are given here to facilitate reading the text, but it has not been possible to include here the rich level of detail provided by Borbone's annotations published there. In a small number of cases, corrections have been introduced into the translation in consultation with Borbone's Syriac edition, so it is hoped that this text might be useful to a broad audience, and especially for students, but for researchers it cannot replace Borbone and Parodi's 2021 translation. If this publication introduces more people to the astonishing story of two eastern Turkic Christian monks, who traveled from China to the Middle East and (in Rabban Sawma's case) even to western Europe, at a time of rapid political and religious change, it will have achieved its purpose.

The History of Mar Yahballaha & Rabban Sawma

By the strength of our Lord Jesus Christ,[1] I begin to write the history of the father of fathers, the lord and chief of the shepherds, Mar Yahballaha, the *catholicos* patriarch of the East,[2] and Rabban Sawma, the general overseer,[3] who were eastern Turks. Lord, help me and bring me to the completion by your mercy. Amen!

Introduction

God, the Lord of all, gracious and merciful, in the abundance of his grace brought everything into existence. In order for humankind to attain from him perfection in the knowledge of truth and in good deeds, to guide the blessed and to direct them to progress, he had his only Son

---

1. It was customary for Eastern Syriac scribes to begin and end copying a text with prayers asking for God's strength to help them finish the job.

2. These are all traditional titles of the head of the Church of the East. Since all clergy were addressed as "father," and bishops addressed as "shepherds," then the patriarch was known as the "father of fathers" and the "chief of the shepherds," as well as their "lord," i.e., the one who governs them. "Mar" itself is an honorific title meaning "my lord," while "*catholicos*" is a title derived from Greek used for the head bishop with authority over everyone else, and "patriarch of the East" contrasts with the various patriarchs of "the West" (i.e., the Mediterranean basin).

3. A "general overseer" (Syriac *sāʿōrā gāwānāyā*) is a church official entrusted with the authority to act as a representative of a bishop, metropolitan, or *catholicos*, but without being tied to particular administrative functions.

descend, who clothed himself in flesh and concealed his glory. Behind the veil of humankind his light shone bright. He abolished material laws, defective and coarse, and decreed spiritual commandments, perfect and pure. By offering his body and his blood he put an end to animal sacrifices and enriched the whole world with the wisdom of his knowledge. He then spread the net of the life-giving gospel through the work of his disciples in every place and region, and scattered the good seed of his proclamation over the whole earth. After them, their own disciples enlightened the four quarters of creation. They were enlightened by the orthodox confession of the majestic Trinity, and have begun to shine in their excellent conduct and perfect practices.

This word is not unacceptable or incredible, since the Lawgiver himself had guaranteed and confirmed it, saying, "Behold, I am with you always until the end of the world."[4] To the promise was added its fulfillment, and to the word was added the action, step by step, until he made the lawless ones God's children, for the Indians, the Chinese, and the other eastern peoples from various lands were constrained;[5] they received the bridle of the fear of God, and their senses and minds were anointed by the Spirit.

In fact, a noble family is worth nothing when thoughts and conduct do not conform to what is good; nor is the gift withheld when an ignoble family is coupled with good conduct and right thoughts. What good came to the Jews from their being of Abraham's offspring, when they renounced the household of God? What did it matter for Gentiles, when they received this and were brought into the household? Today the Turks have bent their necks to the yoke of divine authority and wholeheartedly believed and approved the word of the Lord: "Everyone who does not leave his father, mother, wife, children, brothers, and sisters, and does not bear his cross, and come after me, is not worthy to be my disciple."[6]

4. Matthew 28:20.

5. This describes the conversion to Christianity of people in India, China, and "the East" as something God caused to happen, and "the fear of God" is being compared to a horse's bridle.

6. Matthew 10:37–38; Luke 14:26–27.

Hearing this perfect commandment immediately amazed the two valiant men this story is going to speak about. They cast off their desires, they neglected their parents and children, in short they rejected all the advantages of their own upbringing, and like swift eagles they renewed the youth of their thoughts by wearisome labors and laborious conduct, until they reached what they had constantly hoped for, and from the labors which they planted, they gained desirable and delicious fruits as perfect nourishment.

We[7] shall therefore speak separately about the family of each one of them, their country, the form of their individual upbringing, and both the sojourning and the monastic life they spent together. While telling their history, we shall also write about the things that happened in their time, what happened to them, through them, or because of them, and we shall tell everything just as it happened.

First, the Background of Rabban Sawma

There was a Christian nobleman, God-fearing, wealthy in the things of the world and in the things of nature,[8] from a distinguished lineage and family. His name was Shiban, the administrator of the church, and he lived in the city called Khanbaliq,[9] that is, the capital of the eastern region. He was legally married to a woman named Qyamta,[10] and since time had passed without an heir being born to them, they persisted in supplication and prayer to God, so that he would not deprive them of

7. The author uses "we" to refer to himself.

8. I.e., he not only owned a lot of property, but also had good health and talents.

9. Shiban (or Sheban) is a Mongol personal name. Khanbaliq (modern Beijing) means "city of the khan" (i.e., the Mongol ruler), and it was founded as the capital of Mongol rule in China in 1264. Since the city was not founded when Sawma was born, this is an anachronism that serves to tie Sawma to the Mongol imperial leadership.

10. Qyamta is a Syriac name meaning "resurrection" (also used as the name of Easter).

one to continue their family and console them. God, then, in his kindness and love, accepted their request and had mercy on them, for he is inclined to accept the plea of the broken-hearted and to hear the cry of those who plead and make requests, for "everyone that asks receives; and he that seeks finds, and to him who knocks it shall be opened,"[11] he said confidently, based on solid hope. In fact, it works for both sexes, that is, of men and women, when they put forward requests with righteous intentions. Indeed, Hannah, the wife of Elkanah, was not rejected when she prayed with a righteous purpose, and Manoah's wife was not driven out when she promptly received the angel in her chamber.[12]

He breathed a spirit of conception into the woman,[13] and she gave birth to a son who was named Sawma; they were very happy indeed, and their neighbors and relatives rejoiced over his birth. They raised him in a praiseworthy manner to an age suitable for him to begin to learn; they then entrusted him to a suitable teacher and in his presence they instructed him carefully in church doctrines. They arranged his marriage and rejoiced in him. He was deemed worthy of the rank of priests,[14] and he was numbered among the clerical ranks. He became a custodian in the church of the city mentioned. His conducted himself with all chastity and humility; zealous in acquiring virtues, he worked hard to attain the life of the things to come[15] until he was twenty years old. Then divine fire kindled in his heart, burned up the thorns of sin, and purified his shining soul from filth and all vileness. Indeed, he cherished the love of his Lord above everything else, and had no intention to look back after putting his hand to the plough.[16] He cast aside the shadow of this world at once,

---

11. Matthew 7:8.

12. 1 Samuel 1; Judges 13.

13. This is an unusual way to say that God caused Qyamta to become pregnant.

14. In the Church of the East, priests are allowed to marry, though monks are not.

15. I.e., he lived in light of the idea that God would judge things and bring rewards to the blessed.

16. Cf. Luke 9:62.

and he immediately rejected its delights. Pungent meals were as good as nonexistent to him, and he entirely refused intoxicating beverages.

When his parents realized this, they were deeply saddened, afflicted by lasting pain at the thought that their only child would leave them. With a broken heart, they began to plead and entice him with worldly promises: "Why, dear son, does separating from us seem good to you? How can you delight in our affliction? Why is our grief sweet to you? Consider: to whom will our property be left? Ponder: where is our heir? Reflect: who will possess our work? How can it please you that our offspring and name will be wiped out? How can your plan suggest that strangers will become our heirs?" When with tears they pleaded with him in these ways, with their crying out they distressed him with similar reasoning. He obeyed them at least outwardly and he remained with them bodily, not according to his will, and while for three years he served his biological parents, he did not stop his labor and he constantly worked hard in his difficult course.[17]

When they realized that their urging was useless because their words were considered nothing compared to his love of Christ, his parents allowed him to fulfill his desires. He then distributed all his property to the poor, that is, his clothes and his things, and he took the habit of monasticism; he received the tonsure[18] from the holy father, the reverend Saint George, the metropolitan, and he began to work in the vineyard of his Lord with his hope fixed on the kingdom to come,[19] confident of possessing a heavenly reward and that he would receive as wages a full *dīnār*.[20] He picked a cell and shut himself into it for seven years,[21] at the end of which he decided to withdraw from humankind and practice

17. This is describing Sawma's continuation of self-discipline to make spiritual progress even while he is outwardly living with his parents.

18. This is describing the process of becoming a monk: giving up all property, putting on a special robe (the habit), and having his head ceremonially shaved (the tonsure).

19. This is a way of describing heaven.

20. Cf. Matthew 20:1–16.

21. One common form of monastic discipline was to enclose oneself in a small room. In the most extreme forms, one might block off the door apart from a small hole for

asceticism in the mountains, in a solitary place, so as to find peace in seclusion. So he set out and, having walked away from their city for a day, he chose to remain there. He found a place with a cave and beside it a spring of water on the mountain. He settled there in peace, thanking the Lord for deeming him worthy of so much. Then the news spread across those lands; people began gathering by him to listen to his words, and honor was assigned to him by everybody.

Background of Mar Yahballaha, the *Catholicos* Patriarch of the East

All is known to the foreknowledge of God, and human purposes, both those of the right hand and those of the left hand,[22] all of them are apparent to him before they are formed in the womb. Therefore he chooses and justifies based on them, and because of them he punishes and tortures. To Moses it was said, "Behold, I have made you a god to Pharaoh";[23] his being chosen makes known the goodness of his will and Pharaoh's hard-heartedness, since even before he came into existence, it was known that he would be hard-hearted, so he could be rejected. For God said to Jeremiah, "Before I formed you in the belly I knew you; and before you came forth out of the womb I sanctified you and I ordained you a prophet to the nations."[24] And Paul said, "God has not driven out his people, which was foreknown by him,"[25] because of their excellent will and their pure intentions.

Some signs of God's choice appear in the chosen person, and a light radiates from him, which proclaims him worthy of divine grace.

---

food to be passed through; in less extreme cases, the monk might be able to leave for bodily functions but would avoid social contact.

22. Cf. Matthew 25:31–46.

23. Exodus 7:1.

24. Jeremiah 1:5.

25. Romans 11:2.

The enlightened one perceives these signs, but the unskilled one remains unaware. Since the subject of this story was chosen to be exalted in course, we are bound to tell the circumstances of his being chosen and how this was proof of a perfect will.

There was in the city of Kosheng, in the East, a believer and a just man, pure and without blemish, who continuously served God in his church and behaved rightly according to divine laws. His name was Bayniel the archdeacon.[26] He had four children, the youngest of whom was called Mark. He was instructed in church doctrine more thoroughly than his brothers.

[...][27]

The guests[?] admonished him for this and for other similar things. In this way it seemed to them that they were speaking to a column,[28] rather than with a rational being. Despite pressures of many kinds, he did not turn from his course, nor did his determination weaken from what he sought, but rather his purpose was straight ahead. He reached Rabban Sawma after a difficult journey, which lasted fifteen days; when he greeted him, Rabban Sawma rejoiced and welcomed him with gladness.

After he had rested, Rabban Sawma asked him, "My son, where are you from? What led you to come to this mountain? Which town is your family from? Who is your father, and whose descendant are you?" He replied, "I am the son of Bayniel the archdeacon, from the city of Kosheng, and my name is Mark." Rabban Sawma said to him, "Why did you come to me, at the price of such labor and disturbance?" Mark

26. The name "Bayniel" is otherwise unknown, and likely corrupted by a scribe from an unfamiliar name. One suggestion is Baynal, and another Bayan-el; for the latter, see Mark Dickens, "Yahbalaha the Turk: An Inner Asian Patriarch of the Eastern Christians," in Mark Dickens, ed., *Echoes of a Forgotten Presence: Reconstructing the History of the Church of the East in Central Asia* (Münster: LIT Verlag, 2020), 284. Without other evidence, it has been left in the form as it occurs in the text.

27. Something seems to have been omitted accidentally from all copies of the Syriac text, which likely explained Mark's decision to join Rabban Sawma. Because of the gap, the interpretation of the next word is uncertain.

28. Compare the English idiom "speaking to a post."

answered him, "I want to be a hermit.[29] Because I heard of you, I left everything to seek you. Please don't deprive me of what I desire." Rabban Sawma told him, "Brother, this is a difficult path, such that the elderly can barely endure its difficulty, let alone youths and boys following it." When he had tried in many ways to persuade him to return to his parents and he did not obey, he eventually took him as a disciple. He clothed him in a woolen robe[30] and took him in his service. After three years Mark received his tonsure, that is, the habit,[31] from the reverend Mar Nestorius the metropolitan, on the Sunday of the hymn *rūḥā pāraqlīṭā*.[32] He persisted with countless labors and daytime fasts. They both practiced asceticism on the mountain, in the service of purity and holiness, and derived comfort from God, to whom they had devoted themselves.

Rabban Sawma and Rabban Mark Resolve to Travel to Jerusalem

One day they thought, "If we leave this land and travel to the West, we would benefit greatly when we receive the blessings of the shrines of the holy martyrs and of the *catholicos* fathers; then if Christ, the Lord of all, prolongs our lives and sustains us with his grace, we might go to Jerusalem in order to obtain a complete atonement for our faults and the remission of our sins."[33] Rabban Sawma held back Rabban Mark,

29. This indicates that Mark wishes to leave ordinary society and live (presumably with Rabban Sawma) in the wilderness as one devoted to God.

30. Wearing a woolen robe is a sign of a monk.

31. Typically "tonsure" refers to shaving the head and "habit" to the robe, so this phrase is awkward, but it indicates the ritual of becoming a monk.

32. This Sunday is six weeks after Pentecost, usually in June, but because the year of this event is unknown a precise date cannot be assigned.

33. "The West" here refers to western Asia, Iraq, and farther west; previous *catholicos* patriarchs were buried in Baghdad. Medieval Christians and Muslims shared the idea that visiting the graves of holy people was a way to gain God's blessing. For Christians, the greatest such pilgrimage was visiting Jerusalem and the Church of the

frightening him with the labors of the journey, the fatigue of the voyage, the fearfulness of the routes, and the stresses of being foreigners. But Rabban Mark burned with desire to go; his thought was revealing to him that some treasures were stored up for him in the West. He was pressing Rabban Sawma with his words, pestering him to depart. When they mutually agreed that neither would leave the other, no matter what trouble he might endure as a result, then they rose and, after distributing to the poor their few belongings and the things of their service, they entered the city in order to find travel companions and prepare provisions. The Christians there at once recognized them, learned about their plans, and gathered around them to turn them back from their plan, saying, "Do you not realize how far it is to the region where you are going? Do you not know how winding and difficult the routes are, and does it escape your notice that you will never get there? Remain here, and pursue the asceticism to which you were called, because it is written, 'The kingdom of God is within you.'"[34] They replied, "We have already put on the robe,[35] and we are dead to the world, having rejected it, so no labor frightens us, and no fear troubles us. One thing we ask of you: that in the love of Christ you pray for us and, setting aside speech which produces uncertainty, you ask God to fulfill our wish." Then the Christians replied, "Go in peace." They kissed each other goodbye, separating with sad crying and pitiful voices while saying, "Go in peace. May our Lord, whom you seek, be with you! May he provide for you what pleases him and helps you! Amen!"

They came to the city of Kosheng. When the inhabitants and the parents of Rabban Mark heard about the arrival of the two hermits, they went out to meet them with joy and welcomed them with gladness and cheerfulness. With all honors they brought them into their church and questioned them, "How was your journey?" For they thought they

---

Resurrection; some Christians, including here Rabban Sawma and Rabban Mark (or the author), connect pilgrimage to Jerusalem with forgiveness of all their sins.

34. Luke 17:21.

35. I.e., as monks.

had come to stay with them and that Rabban Mark had done this to be near his parents. But when it was established that they were going to Jerusalem and had directed their purpose toward the West, and that they were traveling, [the people] were greatly saddened and seriously grieved. News of their arrival reached the lords of the city, the sons-in-law of the king of kings, the *qa'an*, that is, Kun Buqa and Ay Buqa,[36] who, as soon as they heard the news, sent messengers who led the monks to their encampment. They welcomed them with cheerfulness, and burning affection for them was kindled within them. When they heard that they were about to leave, they began to say, "Why are you leaving our land to head West? We work hard to attract monks and spiritual fathers from the West to this region; how can we let you leave?" Rabban Sawma replied, "We have abandoned the world and as long as we are among people, we will have no rest. Therefore, we need to run away for the love of Christ, who gave himself to death in exchange for our salvation. Whatever exists in this world, we have cast behind us; even if your love urges us not to leave, your kindness restrains us, the alms you gave us are so abundant, and even dwelling with you is pleasant to us, yet we remember the saying of the Lord, 'For what does it benefit a person if he gains the whole world and loses his soul? And what shall a person give in exchange for his soul?'[37] Though we desire to leave, wherever we will be and as our weakness allows, day and night we will remember your kingdom in our prayers."

When they realized that speaking with them was useless and they were not swayed by persuasion, the kings presented them with animals to ride, gold, silver, and clothing. But the monks said, "We need nothing. What would we do with possessions? How could we carry such a burden?" The two kings replied, "You are unfamiliar with the length

---

36. *Qa'an* (also spelled *khaghan*) is the Mongol title for the "great khan," here explained by the phrase "king of kings." Kun Buqa had married the daughter of the earlier great khan Güyük (r. 1246–48), and Ay Buqa had married the daughter of the great khan Qubilai (r. 1260–94). They were leaders of the Önggüd Turks, who governed the area of Kosheng.

37. Matthew 16:26.

of this journey and the expenses it entails. But we know, and we advise you not to leave empty-handed: otherwise, you will not be able to reach your destination. Therefore, accept these gifts from us as a loan: if you are forced by necessity, spend them; and if you arrive in good health, distribute them among the monasteries and the convents of the monks of that land and the fathers, so that with them we may have a connection with our fathers in the West. It is said: 'Your abundance may be a supply for their want.'"[38]

When the monks saw that the kings' offer came from a sincere heart, they accepted what those kings gave them. They left each other deeply moved, and tears mixed with joy accompanied them.

From there they reached the city of Tangut.[39] The inhabitants of that city had heard that Rabban Sawma and Rabban Mark had come on their way to Jerusalem. They went out to greet them with enthusiasm, both men and women, youths, teenagers, children, and infants, for the faith of the people of Tangut was fervent and their intention was pure. They honored them with all kinds of presents and received blessings. The crowd accompanied them, weeping and saying, "May our Lord who chose you for the honor of serving him be with you, amen!"

From there they went to the region of Khotan, after two months of struggle and hardship in that empty desert. Nobody lives there because of its bitter water; nothing can be planted there, and along the entire way there are only about eight days during which drinking water can be found to support travelers. At the time of their arrival in Khotan there had just been a conflict between the king of kings, the *qa'an*, and King Hoqu.[40] The latter, having escaped from the *qa'an*, had arrived there, where he had slaughtered thousands of people. The roads and tracks

38. 2 Corinthians 8:14.

39. Tangut (also called Xi Xia) was a region, so it is unclear which city this would have been, though various suggestions have been made.

40. This name probably refers to the son of the earlier great khan Güyük (r. 1246–48), who had supported Ariq-böke's side of the civil war against Qubilai but then was pardoned and sent to Turkistan after the latter's victory. A Chinese document from 1276 mentions the difficulty of traveling along this route due to Hoqu's rebellion.

were cut off,[41] grain was lacking and could not be found, and many died in the famine. After six months, the monks left that place and went to Kashgar.[42] They found the city depopulated, as it had been looted by enemies for some time. But because their purpose was determined and they were pleasing God with their whole heart, he averted every danger from them and no suffering met them, and he rescued them from captors and robbers. They arrived before King Qaidu in Talas and were received by him.[43] Praying for his life and blessing his kingdom, they asked him for a command that no one would harm them within his territory. They reached Khorasan with difficulty, worn out by incessant fear, and deprived of most of their belongings along the way.[44] They arrived at the holy monastery of venerable Zion, near the city of Tus. They were blessed by the bishop and the monks of that place, and they thought it was like being born again to the world. They thanked God, in whom they had trusted; in him they had hoped, and they were delivered,[45] for he is the supporter and helper of everyone who seeks him.

41. This means that it was impossible to travel without being attacked by an army.

42. Kashgar was normally a major city along the "Silk Road," and it was also a center of Christianity.

43. Qaidu was the most powerful Mongol ruler of Central Asia at this time, and he did not submit to the *qa'an* Qubilai. Talas (modern Taraz, Kazakhstan) is a town on the steppe north of the Tien Shan Mountains.

44. Medieval travel was much more difficult than modern travel, even beyond the physical exertion of riding or walking long distances for many months. Most non-nomads traveling needed to purchase enough food and water to travel between major cities and bring it along. The fear of robbers attacking a group of travelers, taking away any valuables they can find (including enslaving people), led many travelers to hire security guards to protect the caravan from robbers, but they were expensive and one never knew if one had hired enough. Any belongings that were not lost to robbers or guards might be demanded as "road tolls" or expected as gifts by local rulers and regional governors along the way.

45. Cf. Psalm 22:4–5.

When they had been refreshed by the company of their brothers there, they set off for Azerbaijan,[46] from which they were going to travel to the *catholicos* Mar Denha in Baghdad. But as it turned out, the lord *catholicos* had gone to Maragha,[47] so they met him there. Their joy was great, and their gladness increased; their minds were calmed, and they rested from their purpose at the sight of him. They fell to the ground before him, prostrating themselves with tears, and it was as if they had seen our Lord Jesus Christ in the person of Mar Denha the *catholicos* (may his memory be blessed). Then they said to him, "His love for us is great, and his grace is poured out upon us, since we see the glorious and spiritual face of our universal father!"[48] When he asked them, "Where do you come from?" they replied, "We came from the East, from Khanbaliq, the city of the king of kings, the *qa'an*, to be blessed by you, by the fathers, the monks and the saints of this region. Then, if we have a way and God has mercy on us, we will go to Jerusalem." When the *catholicos* saw their tears mixed with the joy of meeting him, he was moved with compassion for them and comforted them with these words, "Truly, my sons, may the guardian angel protect you in this difficult journey and be a guide for you until the fulfillment of your request. Do not be afflicted by your labors, because he says by the prophet,[49] 'Those who sow in tears shall reap in joy.'[50] May you arrive at what you hope for and, in exchange for suffering and pain, you will receive in this world a full reward and double wages, and in the world to come, good things that will not fail and bliss that will not cease." Bowing before him, they thanked him.

46. This region is larger than the modern country of this name; it includes what is today northwestern Iran.

47. Baghdad, in Iraq, was the headquarters of the Church of the East before the Mongol period, but the Mongols ruled Iraq and Iran from the city of Maragha, located in southern part of the Azerbaijan region (today in Iran).

48. I.e., the patriarch.

49. The biblical psalms were traditionally ascribed to David, who was regarded as a prophet by Christians and Muslims.

50. Psalm 126:5.

After enjoying his company for a few days, they presented a request: "If we find favor in our father's eyes, may he allow us to travel to Baghdad, in order to receive a blessing at the holy shrine of Saint Mari the apostle, teacher of the East,[51] and at the shrines of the fathers that are found in that city. From there we shall reach the monasteries in the lands of Beth Garmai and Nisibis,[52] to be blessed and to seek (divine) help." The *catholicos*, seeing how good their intentions were, how sincere their souls were, and how determined their resolve was, said, "Go, my sons; may Christ, the Lord of all, grant your request from his rich and abundant treasury. May he fulfill his grace in you, and may his favor follow you everywhere you go!" He wrote a letter of introduction for them to these places, so they might be honored everywhere they went, and he had a man escort them to show them the way and guide them in the paths.

They arrived in Baghdad, and from there reached the great church of Kokhe. They went to the monastery of Saint Mari the apostle and received blessings from the shrines of that land. Then they turned to Beth Garmai, where they received the blessing of the shrine, full of (divine) help and healings, of Saint Ezekiel. Afterward they left for Arbil, and from there traveled to Mosul. Then they proceeded to Sinjar, Nisibis, and Mardin, and received blessings in the shrine that preserves the bones of Saint Awgen, the "second Christ";[53] then they went to Gazarta of Beth Zabdai. They received blessings from all the shrines, monasteries, convents, monks, and fathers of those provinces. They fulfilled the vows they had previously made, they gave banquets, and they distributed alms wherever they went. Finally, they turned back and went to the holy monastery of Saint Michael of Tarʿel, where they purchased a cell[54] and

51. Syriac tradition names Mari as the first person to preach Christianity in the Parthian Empire, in what is today Iraq.

52. Beth Garmai corresponds to central Iraq, and Nisibis is the city of Nusaybin in Upper Mesopotamia. Both areas were important centers of monasticism in the earlier history of the Church of the East.

53. Syriac tradition names Saint Awgen as the founder of monasticism in Syriac.

54. As monks, Rabban Sawma and Rabban Mark need a monastery to call home, and they paid for a room ("a cell") to be prepared for them to live in.

were welcomed by the monks there. The intention that made them toil on the journey rested, although they had not yet reached the limit of their original goal.

When Mar Denha the *catholicos* heard of their conduct, he sent and required them to come to him. They went at once and gave him the customary greeting. He said to them, "We heard you joined a monastery, but this does not please us, since when you dwell in a monastery, you gain rest for yourselves alone, but when you will be with us, you will contribute to benefit and rest for others. Therefore, stay with us and help at the royal court, for any business that may come to hand." Rabban Sawma and Rabban Mark replied, "Everything that our father commands, we shall do." He said to them, "You will go to King Abaqa.[55] You will receive decrees for us." They replied, "We'll do it. But let the lord our father send a man with us to take the decree and give it to him, while we shall go from there to Jerusalem." He granted them this and provided them with blessings. When they reached the blessed camp, the emirs took them before the king,[56] who asked questions about their arrival and their native land. They answered him something that revealed to him their intention; he then ordered his royal officers to grant their request, and to give them decrees as they required. They sent the decree that the lord *catholicos* sought with his messenger.

They left in the company of others, heading for Jerusalem. When they reached the town of Ani,[57] they came and saw the monasteries and churches there, amazed by the imposing and beautiful buildings. From there they entered Georgia so that they could go by a clear road, but upon arrival the people of that region informed them that the road had been cut off due to murders that had taken place and robbers.

55. Abaqa (r. 1265–82) was the Mongol Ilkhan ruling Iraq, Iran, Anatolia, and Armenia.

56. An emir is a military leader. Here it refers to the Mongol commanders.

57. Ani was a former capital of an Armenian kingdom (now located in eastern Turkey) and it was famous for its many church buildings.

Rabban Mark Is Ordained Metropolitan with the Name of Mar Yahballaha and Rabban Sawma Becomes a General Overseer[58]

They returned to the lord *catholicos*, who rejoiced in them and told them, "This is no time to travel to Jerusalem, because the roads are disturbed and the routes cut off. But you have received blessings from all the houses of God and the shrines within them, and in my opinion, if someone visits them with a sincere heart, their service is not inferior to arriving at Jerusalem.[59] I am giving you useful advice, which you should listen to! I decided to appoint Rabban Mark as metropolitan and to grant the apostolic gift to him;[60] concerning you, Rabban Sawma, I will ordain you general overseer and send both of you back to your native countries." Those monks replied, "What the lord our father says is from the command of Christ, and anyone who does not comply is committing a transgression. But in this case, we will reveal our thoughts and make known what is hidden in our heart. We have not come from there to return there again, and we do not think we could endure again a second time all the hardship we endured: indeed, only a fool will stumble on the same stone twice. Besides, we say that we are unworthy of this gift, and an office like this is too difficult for simple men. All we ask for is this: to remain in the monastery, serving Christ until we die." The *catholicos* said to them, "The gift is fitting for you, and the office suited to your modesty." When they saw that no excuses could be made, they said, "Let our father's will be done." The *catholicos* said, "So far there has been no metropolitan

58. A "general overseer" (Syriac *sāʿōrā gāwānāyā*) is a church official entrusted with the authority to act as a representative of a bishop, metropolitan, or *catholicos*, but without being tied to particular administrative functions.

59. The spiritual value of pilgrimage to Jerusalem was debated, and some thought that local shrines were just as good, while others thought the pure desire to go was as valuable as actually arriving.

60. Ordination as bishop (here including metropolitan, a form of archbishop) was thought to confer the spiritual gift of being heir to the apostles (leaders among Jesus's earliest followers).

by the name of Mar Mark. I would be glad to call Rabban Mark that, although I also planned this, that we would write down suitable names and put them on the altar; the name drawn by the hand of the one who is going to bear it, that name we shall give him." So they did, and the name was Yahballaha.[61] The *catholicos* said, "This is from the Lord, may he always be blessed!" They agreed, and Rabban Mark received the rank of metropolitan from the *catholicos* Mar Denha at the age of thirty-five, for the diocese of Katai and Ong.[62] Rabban Sawma also received the *catholicos*'s blessing and was named general overseer. Both received letters of credentials, each according to his office.

A few days later it became known that the route by which they had come from China was entirely cut off, and no one was traveling on it, because the attitude of the kings of bordering regions on the shores of the Jayhun River had changed.[63] Therefore, the two illumined ones returned to the monastery of Saint Michael of Tarʿel, where they lived in their cell for about two years.

One night, during his sleep, Mar Yahballaha dreamed that he had entered a great church. In that church were images of saints, and among them was a cross.[64] He stretched out his right arm to be blessed, and the more he stretched it out, the longer the arm became, and the higher the cross rose, until it reached the top of the sanctuary; there he took hold of it and kissed it. Stepping out of the church, he saw tall trees filled with various kinds of fruit. He began picking them and eating, and giving and providing them to the crowd that had gathered there. When he woke up, he told Rabban Sawma, "I had a dream that disturbed me." Rabban Sawma said to him, "Tell it to me." After he told him the dream, Rabban

61. It was customary for bishops to be renamed when they were consecrated.

62. A diocese is the region for which a bishop is responsible. Katai refers to northern China, and Ong to the region inhabited by the Önggüd people in Inner Mongolia.

63. This is referring to conflict between the Ilkhanate and the Chaghatai Khanate, whose border lay along the Jayhun River (known to the ancient Greeks as the Oxus, known today as the Amu Darya).

64. In the medieval period, the Church of the East had icons—images of saints in their churches.

Sawma interpreted it, saying, "The fact that your arm grew long when you stretched it out to obtain a blessing from the cross and the images of the saints means you shall reach the great stature of the fathers. The fruits you were eating from the trees and giving the people to eat mean that the heavenly gift that rests upon you and that you enjoy will give joy to many others." On another night, Mar Yahballaha had another vision, like one seated on an elevated throne, and a large crowd gathered around him as he was teaching. As he spoke, his tongue was growing until much of it came out of his mouth, then it split into three tips, and on each something like a fire appeared. The people around him were amazed and glorifying God. When he awoke, he told the vision to Rabban Sawma, who said to him, "Rather than a dream, this has all the characteristics of a revelation, and it is in no way different from the Spirit who rested upon the apostles in the likeness of tongues of fire![65] The Holy Spirit has rested upon you too. The throne of the patriarchate will be entrusted to your hands, to fulfill its ministry and to minister its service."

Mar Yahballaha Is Elected Patriarch

As these events were taking place, Mar Denha the *catholicos* was still alive, but he was suffering from illness in Baghdad. Many other monks and fathers were having similar dreams.[66] A few days later, Mar Yahballaha resolved to go and see the *catholicos* in Baghdad to receive his blessing, the cloak and staff that he was to take with him to his region.[67] As he approached Baghdad, he met an acquaintance who said to him, "The *catholicos* has died, but maybe if you push your animal onward,[68]

65. Acts 2:2–4.

66. The text is unspecific whether these other dreams predicted Yahballaha's election as *catholicos*, or the selection of the various dreamers, but the former is more likely given genre considerations.

67. The special cloak and staff were signs of his rank as a metropolitan bishop.

68. The term is for a pack animal.

you will arrive in time for the funeral." And so, deeply saddened and brokenhearted, he hastened there until he reached the gate of the church. As he stepped in, he saw a large gathering of people who were weeping, and others who were praying. Walking up to the bier, he threw his turban to the ground and, tearing his clothes, he wept sadly and bitterly, until he fell to the ground like one dead.[69] After a while they put him back on his feet, put the turban back on his head, and comforted him. As the funeral service was over, Mar Denha (may his memory be a blessing) was buried, and the fathers returned to the patriarch's residence.

The following day the fathers gathered to elect a person suitable to sit on the patriarchal throne. Among them were, first, Maran ʿAmmeh, the metropolitan of Elam, and the one of Tangut, the one of Tirhan, and the one of the mountains;[70] with them were the great men, chiefs, scribes, lawyers, and physicians of Baghdad. One put forward a suggestion, another made a different one; finally, they all agreed that Mar Yahballaha should become the head and leader of the patriarchal throne of Seleucia and Ctesiphon.[71] They chose him for this reason: the kings who held the rudder of government in the entire inhabited world were Mongols, and there was no one acquainted with their customs, their way of life, and their language except him. When they told him these things, he objected to their proposition, using such excuses as, "I lack education and church doctrine, and my tongue is limited. How can I do this? Besides, I also do not know your Syriac language, and that is an essential requirement!" But when they pressed him with persuasive arguments, he agreed to their idea and accepted. He was elected unanimously by the bishops, priests, great men, scribes, and even the physicians of Baghdad. He left and went to the holy monastery of Saint Michael of Tarʿel, to see Rabban Sawma. The monks had already heard of the passing away of

69. These are actions signifying his deep grief.

70. These are leaders of the Church of the East.

71. Seleucia and Ctesiphon were the twin capitals of the Sasanian Persian Empire (before the rise of Islam), and the patriarchal office continued to be known by their names.

the holy father Mar Denha; when Mar Yahballaha arrived, they received him with joy and encouraged him, and they agreed that he should be the *catholicos*.

The impulse was divine, and the entire creation necessarily serves to fulfill the outcome that is from him.[72]

Mar Yahballaha spoke to Rabban Sawma, who told him, "This is something divine, and you cannot avoid it. We shall therefore go to King Abaqa and, if he agrees, we have confirmation."

They arose and set off for Azerbaijan together with the bishops, the fathers, and the monks who accompanied them; at the time, the kings used to spend the summer there. They arrived before the king at the Black Mountain, known in Persian as Siyah Kuh. The emirs introduced them and presented their petition, declaring, "May the king live forever! The *catholicos* has died, and all the Christians agreed unanimously that he should be replaced by this metropolitan, who came from the lands of the East to travel to Jerusalem. What does the king command?" He replied, "This purity of purpose and conscience is amazing! God is with those who seek him and those who accomplish his will. This man and his companion came from the East to go to Jerusalem. What happened to them was by God's will. We also serve the divine will and the wishes of the Christians. May he stand as their chief and sit on the patriarchal throne." He took Mar Yahballaha by the hand and told him, "Be strong and lead. May God be with you and help you!" He covered his head with the hood (it was lowered down around his shoulders) and gave him his own seat, which was a small throne, and a parasol, called *sukur* in Mongolian, which is only raised over the heads of kings, queens, and their children, to stop the force of the sun and rain upon them, but most of all to honor them.[73] He was given a *paiza* (that is, the sign of those kings) and the customary

72. The author here ascribes the election of Mar Yahballaha to God's providence.

73. The actions in this sentence convey that the Mongol ruler is honoring Mar Yahballaha greatly, while the following sentence describes Mar Yahballaha receiving his authority from the Ilkhan.

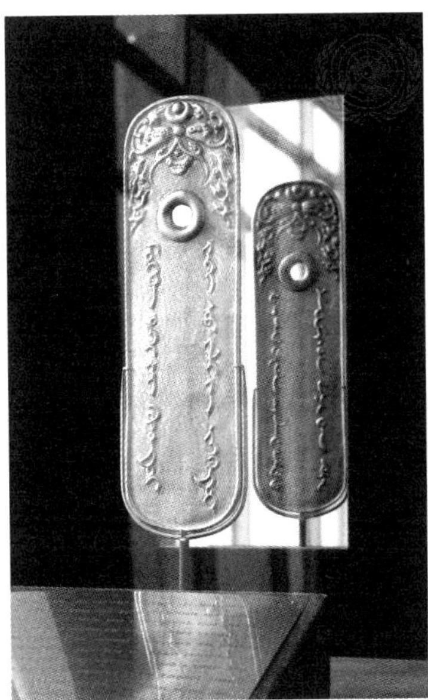

A *paiza* was a tablet that when granted to people conferred rights to use the Mongol postal system (*yam*). The most valuable *paizas* were made of gold, like this one, which is almost a foot long and over three inches wide. *Paizas* made of silver or wood granted fewer usage rights. This one was donated to the United Nations by the government of Mongolia.

decrees that granted him full powers, along with the large seal that had belonged to the preceding *catholicos*.[74] The king also provided the large sums required to cover the cost of his ordination.

They departed for Baghdad, and once there, they went to the great church of Kokhe. Mar Yahballaha received his *cheirotonia* (that is, his ordination),[75] so he could hold the rudder of government of the Church of the East. He sat on the patriarchal throne of Seleucia and Ctesiphon by the mediation of the holy father Maran ʿAmmeh, metropolitan of Elam, the one who ordains and the keeper of the apostolic throne,[76] and the fathers who were present. These were Mar Ishoʿzka, the metropolitan of Soba and Armenia; Mar Mushe, the metropolitan of Arbil;

74. "Customary decrees" refers to a Mongol *yarligh* granting authority to the *catholicos* in his office. A *paiza* is a metal tablet conferred by the Ilkhan that grants certain standard privileges to the person who carries it.

75. The author uses the Greek word first to demonstrate his fancy education.

76. In the Church of the East, a new *catholicos* is ordained by the metropolitan of Elam, who is responsible for administering the patriarchal office ("keeper of the throne") between the death of one *catholicos* and the ordination of his successor.

Mar Gabriel, the metropolitan of Mosul and Nineveh; Mar Eliya, the metropolitan of Daqoq and Beth Garmai; Mar Abraham, the metropolitan of Tripoli and Jerusalem; Mar Yaʿqob, the metropolitan of Samarkand; and Mar Yohannan, the metropolitan of Azerbaijan, along with the remaining bishops, twenty-four in all.[77] The ordination took place in November, on the first Sunday of the Sanctification of the Church, in the Greek year 1593 [November 2, 1281]; he was thirty-seven years old.

It so happened that during the winter of that year, King Abaqa came to Baghdad. Mar Yahballaha the *catholicos* went before him on the Saturday preceding the Lord's Fast [February 7, 1282],[78] to make known to him the situation of the Christians. He found favor before the eyes of the king, who lavished great gifts on him and decreed for his sake that every year he should receive thirty thousand *dīnār*s, the equivalent of 180,000 white *zūzē*,[79] for the churches, monasteries, monks, priests, and deacons. The *catholicos* subsequently sent people to collect this donation from various regions. But when the king departed from temporal life, the donation was stopped.[80]

---

77. The Arabic biography of Mar Yahballaha III in the *Kitāb Asfār al-asrār* lists twenty-two metropolitans and bishops present, including Mar Ishoʿsabran of Tangut named later in this text, but omitting Mar Yaʿqob of Samarkand and Mar Yohannan of Azerbaijan named here. Ṣalībā Ibn Yūḥannā al-Mawṣilī, *Asfār al-asrār III: Livre cinquième*, ed. Gianmaria Gianazza (Beirut: Éditions du CEDRAC, 2024), 476–77.

78. "The Lord's Fast" refers to Lent, the season of fasting before Easter.

79. *Dīnār*s were the high-value silver coins of the Ilkhanate, but the author converts the sum into the more commonly used "white *zūzē*," that is, silver *dirhams*.

80. "Temporal life" means "mortal life," as contrasted with "eternal life," so this is a euphemism for Abaqa dying. Since the annual stipend was a gift of Abaqa, when he died, the gift ceased.

False Accusations Against Mar Yahballaha in King Ahmad's Time

We shall not dwell on what happened in the meantime: that king was replaced by his brother, called Ahmad,[81] the son of King Hülegü. Lacking education and knowledge, he persecuted Christians harshly by his fellowship with Hagarenes[82] and his inclination toward them.

Then two envious bishops took the opportunity to carry out their wishes:[83] they went before King Ahmad through the intercession of some Muslims, one of whom was called Shams al-Din and was the head of the *dīwān* (that is, the treasury's head scribe) and the other was Shaykh ʿAbd al-Rahman.[84] The two slandered Mar Yahballaha the *catholicos* and Rabban Sawma and accused them: "In their hearts they favor Arghun, son of Abaqa, and they wrote to the king of kings, the *qaʾan*, to complain against you; this accusation has been joined by the emir Yoshmut." At that time, the latter was governor of the city of Mosul and its district; he had been a monk and an ascetic.[85] The two people mentioned thereby

81. Better known in English by his Mongol name, Tegüder.

82. I.e., Muslims. Hagar is a character in the biblical book of Genesis (chapters 16 and 21), where she was a slave held by Abraham's wife Sarah and the mother of Abraham's son Ishmael, and Muslims were called Hagarenes because medieval people believed that the Arabs were descended from Ishmael and Hagar (even though many Muslims in the Mongol Ilkhanate were not Arabs). Other Christian sources record Ahmad Tegüder's favor toward Christians, so the claim that he persecuted Christians probably reflects the author's own anti-Muslim bias and his desire to glorify Ghazan, whose father Arghun rebelled against and deposed Ahmad Tegüder (see below).

83. Two bishops attempted to get Mar Yahballaha deposed or executed by accusing him before the ruler.

84. The former was the vizier Shams al-Din Juvayni, and the latter was a powerful advisor of Ahmad Tegüder.

85. Yoshmut was an Uyghur ambassador sent by Qubilai to Abaqa in the mid-1270s, who was appointed by the latter to government positions in the Ilkhanate. The text mentions his former religious lifestyle (being a monk, engaging in unspecified forms

turned Ahmad into a tool to achieve their goals, through the said bishops, who were Isho'sabran, metropolitan of Tangut, and Simon, bishop of Arni. They had agreed that one was to become *catholicos* and the other metropolitan and general overseer, and when, at the devil's suggestion, this plan came to their minds, they acted in the way we have told. The king, who lacked discipline because he had strayed from God, did not consider that these men were acting in their own interests, or wonder what brought them to put forward their accusations, but he believed the deceivers' words. By his command Mar Yahballaha the *catholicos* and Rabban Sawma were brought to court along with the emir Yoshmut, and the decrees previously issued concerning the house of the lord *catholicos*, as well as the *paiza*, were confiscated.

As they entered the court hall, they did not know what was demanded of them and were astonished: "What have we done?" The messenger who had led them to court said to them, "Your bishops, the scribes, and confidants are accusing you before the king." Then the great emirs, that is, the judges, asked the *catholicos*, "What evil did you see in the king, which led you to act treacherously toward him and send an accusation to the king of kings, the *qa'an*, saying that he strayed from the path of his ancestors and became a Hagarene?" The *catholicos* replied, "I don't understand!" They said to him, "Your scribes said this about you." They had led them in and interrogated them one at a time, so that each one of them answered what he knew. The lord *catholicos* said, "Emirs, why are you working so hard? Bring back the messenger with whom the letters were sent and examine them. If the accusation against me is confirmed, let me die without mercy, in my own blood. If not, it is up to you to judge and punish." The emirs accepted this proposal and informed the king, who sent for the messenger; they reached him in the area of Khorasan, and all the documents were brought back. When the papers were opened and read out, nothing was found in them that would justify an accusation at all. But the judges did not say anything against the

---

of self-denial called asceticism), which is very unusual for an emir, apparently in order to strengthen the idea that this was an anti-Christian movement.

accusers: from this it is clear that they had used them as a pretext. The *catholicos* thus remained in prison for about forty days, in severe adversity, bitter suffering, and daily affliction, until God in his mercy visited him, saving him from death. King Ahmad was furious with him, and like a thirsty man who is craving water, he was longing to shed his blood; but the guardian angel who protected the holy patriarchal throne, used the king's mother[86] and the emirs and restrained him from the purpose he had made. Through the intercession of these we have mentioned, the *catholicos* found mercy in the eyes of the king, and he gave him the decree and *paiza*, consoled him, and restored him to office.

Then the *catholicos* left the king to go to the city of Urmia. In the church of Saint Mary, he had a dream, and he knew he would never see the king again. After a while he arrived in the city of Maragha, with the bishops who had accused him.

King Ahmad, meanwhile, had gone with his army to Khorasan to capture King Arghun,[87] the son of King Abaqa. He had agreed with the two people we mentioned[88] and the leaders of the Muslims that, once Arghun had been seized, he would kill the other princes and become caliph in Baghdad. Then he would also take the life of the *catholicos*. But his plan came to nothing and his idea was useless. The Lord indeed overcomes the schemes of humanity and establishes his own idea; he confirms kings and removes kings, and his own kingdom stands forever. Ahmad's troops were scattered, and most of them deserted to Arghun, but he was captured and killed.

One night, before the news was heard of what had happened to King Ahmad, Mar Yahballaha the *catholicos* had a dream, as if a handsome youth came toward him, a plate covered by a napkin in his hands, and told him to rise and eat what was in it. When he removed the napkin, he saw a boiled head. He ate it all, leaving only the jawbones. Then

---

86. Ahmad Tegüder's mother was Qutui Khatun, who was a Christian.

87. Notice the anachronism: Arghun was not yet king. This account blames Tegüder for Arghun's rebellion.

88. I.e., the vizier Shams al-Din Juvayni and Shaykh ʿAbd al-Rahman.

the youth asked him, "Do you know what you ate?" He replied, "No." The youth told him, "This was the head of King Ahmad." Suddenly the *catholicos* woke up afraid. A few days later, the news came of his destruction, and that King Arghun had become king. The *catholicos* was very happy, not because of the death of the one, but because of the reign of the other.

In those days he went with the bishops and monks, to bless King Arghun and fulfill the duties of the Christians toward their kings, following the apostle's command, "Let every soul be subject to authorities of greatness. For there is no authority which is not from God."[89] The *catholicos* thus saw King Arghun and blessed him, praying for the establishment of his reign. The king increased his honor and exalted his position, when he learned what had happened to him at the hands of the king who was before him, including the story of those bishops whom we mentioned, which was reported to him. He commanded their execution, but Mar Yahballaha the *catholicos* said, "May the king live forever! As Christians, we have our own laws, and anyone who does not observe them is regarded as a transgressor. Our law does not require anyone to be put to death, but simply punished. There are many kinds of punishments, and those who discipline wrongdoers use them. For these bishops, death is not a suitable penalty in our law; they should instead be entirely deprived of that rank whose ministry they were entrusted with."[90] This pleased the king, who sent off the *catholicos* with great honor, and with joy he returned to the patriarchal residence, with great cheerfulness.

When our fathers the bishops assembled before the *catholicos* to greet him and comfort him, there was an investigation into the story of those bishops mentioned. They made a decision after in-depth investigation and after they confessed their sin: they deposed the two of them, who were removed from all ranks of the church.

89. Romans 13:1.

90. Mar Yahballaha recommends removing them from their office as bishops rather than executing them.

Rabban Sawma's Journey to the Land of the Romans on Behalf of King Arghun and of the *Catholicos* Mar Yahballaha

Mar Yahballaha the *catholicos* was growing in the king's esteem, and day after day he was honored more and more by the kings and queens. He demolished the church of Saint Shallita in Maragha and rebuilt it at great expense; in place of a wooden structure, he made it a double-aisled building, and beside it he made a residence he could live in. The *catholicos* had the greatest affection for the house of King Arghun because the king loved Christians wholeheartedly.

The king was considering the conquest and submission of the lands of Palestine and Syria, but he thought, "If the kings of the West who are Christian do not help me, my wish will not be fulfilled." He therefore asked the *catholicos* to recommend a wise man, suitable and capable of serving as ambassador, so that he could send him to those kings. When the lord *catholicos* saw that no one was as eloquent in speech as Rabban Sawma, who possessed the ability for this, he commanded him to go.

The Journey of Rabban Sawma to the Land of the Romans

Rabban Sawma said, "I want this and desire it!" King Arghun immediately wrote for him decrees addressed to the king of the Greeks and the Franks, that is, the Romans,[91] *yarlighs*,[92] letters, and gifts for each

91. Here "Greeks" refers to the Byzantine Empire, which was the continuation of the Roman Empire (and called itself "Roman"), while "Franks" refers to any western Europeans (including the people of Rome itself along with other western Europeans). In the rest of this text "Romans" sometimes refers to the Byzantine Empire and sometimes to western Europeans.

92. This is the Mongol word for "edicts," which were often granted to recognize a lesser authority.

king. He gave Rabban Sawma two thousand gold *mithqals*,[93] thirty good riding animals, and a *paiza*. Rabban Sawma went to the patriarchal residence to obtain a letter from Mar Yahballaha the *catholicos* as well, and to say goodbye. The *catholicos* gave him permission to go, but when the time of separation came, he was displeased, for he said, "How can this be? You were the administrator of the residence, and you know that with your departure my affairs will get confused!" After he said words like these, they separated from each other with weeping. The *catholicos* sent letters and presents to the pope with him, gifts according to his ability.

Rabban Sawma in Constantinople

Rabban Sawma left, accompanied by some excellent priests and deacons from the patriarchal residence. He arrived in the land of the Romans, on the near shores of the sea,[94] and saw the church there. He boarded a ship, and his companions with him. On the ship were more than three hundred people, and each day he encouraged them with a sermon on the faith. Most of the people on that ship were Romans, and because of his eloquence, they honored him more than a little.

After a few days he arrived at the great city of Constantinople. Before entering the city, he sent two youths to the king's gate, to announce the arrival of the ambassador of King Arghun. The king ordered people to come out to greet them and to lead them into the city with pomp and honor. When Rabban Sawma entered the city, a house was assigned to him, that is, a residence for his stay. Once he had rested, Rabban Sawma went before the king *basileus*.[95] After greeting him, the king asked, "How are you, after the troubles of the sea and the weariness of the journey?"

93. Gold coins weighing about 4.5 g each.

94. The "near shores of the sea" most likely refers to the Black Sea at Trebizond, the easternmost Greek state.

95. *Basileus* is the Greek word for "king" or "emperor"; the Syriac text gives the title "king" in Syriac, followed by a transcription of the Greek title. It is unclear whether

He replied, "With the sight of a Christian king the weariness vanished and the trouble disappeared! I very much hoped to see your kingdom (may our Lord preserve it)!"

After enjoying food and drink, he requested permission from the king to see the churches and the shrines of the patriarchate, and the saints' relics found there.[96] The king entrusted Rabban Sawma to the great men of his kingdom, who showed him all that was there. First, he went to the great church of Hagia Sophia,[97] which has 360 gates, all finished with marble. It is impossible to describe the dome above the altar to someone who has not seen it, or to tell how tall and large it is. In that church is an image of Saint Mary, painted by Luke the Evangelist. He also saw the hand of John the Baptist, relics of Lazarus and Mary Magdalene,[98] and even the stone that was placed on the tomb of our Lord, when the councilor Joseph took him down from the cross.[99] Mary cried on that stone; to this day the spot where her tears fell is wet, and no matter how much that moisture is wiped off, it becomes wet again. He also saw the stone jar, in which our Lord changed water into wine in Cana of Galilee;[100] the reliquary of a holy woman, which is carried in procession every year

---

Rabban Sawma or the Syriac author considered the Greek word to be a name. At this time the emperor was Andronikos II.

96. Constantinople (modern Istanbul) is the seat of one of the ancient patriarchates, regarded by the Church of the East as equal in rank to their own *catholicos* patriarchs. European Christians had collected (or invented) many items that they associated with Jesus or the saints, called relics, which could be body parts of dead saints (e.g., the hand of John the Baptist below) or items that a saint used during their lifetime (e.g., the stone jar). These relics might be encased in protective and decorative containers called reliquaries. Just as Rabban Sawma and Rabban Mark sought out the shrines around Iraq to receive blessings from visiting them, so also in Europe Rabban Sawma was particularly interested in visiting and documenting the relics.

97. The main cathedral in Constantinople. It did not in fact have 360 doors, but more than a hundred.

98. See n. 96 above.

99. This refers to Joseph of Arimathea removing the body of Jesus from the cross and burying him. Cf. Mark 15:43–46.

100. John 2:6–9.

Mosaics in the Hagia Sophia church in Constantinople (modern Istanbul), which Rabban Sawma presumably saw during his visit. Here Emperor Constantine (d. 337), on the right, and Emperor Justinian (d. 565), on the left, present scaled-down images of the churches that they built to the Virgin Mary, who is depicted in the center holding a small Jesus.

and every sick person placed under it will be healed;[101] and also the reliquary of Saint John of the Golden Mouth.[102] He saw the stone on which Simon Peter was seated when the rooster crowed;[103] the tomb of the victorious king Constantine, which is red-colored; the tomb of Justinian, of greenish stone;[104] the meeting place of the 318 fathers, who are all in a great church and their bodies do not decompose, because they confirmed the faith.[105] He visited many other shrines of the holy fathers and saw several talismans and a statue modeled in bronze and stone.

---

101. A reliquary is any container for holding relics. Scholars suggest that this was Saint Theodosia.

102. The Syriac text provides a literal translation of the name of John Chrysostom.

103. Matthew 26:74–75.

104. These are the tombs of Constantine I (r. 306–337) and Justinian I (r. 527–565).

105. This refers to the Council of Nicaea (325), to which 318 bishops reportedly came from across the Roman Empire and agreed on a statement of Christian belief

Finally, Rabban Sawma arrived before the king *basileus* and said, "May the king live forever! I give thanks to our Lord for being considered worthy of seeing these holy temples. Now, with the king's permission, I shall leave to accomplish the command of King Arghun, for the command is to travel to the lands of the Franks." Then the king treated him well and presented him with gifts of gold and silver.

Rabban Sawma in Italy and in Great Rome

He left there to go down to the sea; on the coast he saw a monastery of the Romans, in whose treasury there were two silver reliquaries, one of which contained the head of Saint John of the Golden Mouth, the other that of the pope who baptized King Constantine.[106]

Then he got on a ship and, once out on the open sea, he saw a mountain from which smoke rises all day long, while at night fire appears on it;[107] no one can venture nearby because of the smell of sulfur. People say that there is a great serpent there, and that is why that sea is called Sea of the Dragon.[108] That sea is indeed frightening: many ships full of men have been lost in it.

(the Nicene Creed). Most of those bishops were buried elsewhere, so it is unclear what Rabban Sawma saw on this visit.

106. "John of the Golden Mouth" is John Chrysostom. "The pope who baptized King Constantine" reflects a conflation of Bishop Eusebius of Nicomedia, who in fact baptized Constantine and was buried in Constantinople, and Pope Sylvester, who did not baptize Constantine and was not buried in Constantinople, but medieval tradition replaced Eusebius of Nicomedia with Pope Sylvester as a more orthodox person to have baptized Constantine.

107. This volcano has commonly been identified as Mount Etna, but the description of it rising out of the sea and erupting continuously more closely matches the island Stromboli, as suggested by Fosco Maraini, "Per amor di Gerusalemme: Due cristiani dalla Mongolia a Bordeaux," *L'indice dei libri del mese* 18 (2001): 13.

108. The word "dragon" here (Syriac *attalyā*) is used for the dragon years in the Chinese zodiac, but its resemblance to the name *Italia* (i.e., Italy) probably explains why Rabban Sawma gives "Sea of the Dragon" as the name of the Tyrrhenian Sea.

The island of Stromboli is a continuously active volcano in the Mediterranean Sea near Italy. It best matches the description of the volcano given in Rabban Sawma's account of his travels.

After two months he came ashore, after enduring much trouble, weariness, and anxiety. He disembarked in a city called Naples; the king was called *il re Charles II.*[109] Rabban Sawma arrived before the king to let him know the aim of his visit. He received him gladly and honored him.

There was at the time a struggle between that king and another, called *il re d'Aragon,*[110] whose troops had arrived aboard numerous ships. The army of this king was in battle formation, and they clashed. *Il re*

109. The Syriac text follows "the king" with *Irid Sharlado*. The first word likely represents the Italian *il re* ("the king"), while the second renders the French name Charles II. Charles of Anjou was the king of Naples after 1285, though at the time of Rabban Sawma's visit he was held prisoner by the Aragonese king of Sicily, James II (*il re d'Aragon* below), so Rabban Sawma likely met the son of Charles II, named Charles Martel. This conflict was a key battle (on June 23, 1287) in the War of the Sicilian Vespers (1282–1302).

110. I.e., "the king of Aragon." The Syriac follows "the king" with *Irad Arkon* (*il re d'Aragon*).

d'Aragon defeated the king *il re Charles II*, killed 12,000 of his men, and sank their ships out at sea. During the confrontation, Rabban Sawma and his companions were on the roof of their dwelling and wondered at the customs of the Franks, who did not harm anybody, apart from those doing the fighting.[111]

From there they proceeded overland on horseback. They rode through several cities and villages, and they marveled to see that no valley was empty of buildings. Along the way they heard that the pope had passed away.[112]

After a few days they arrived in great Rome; Rabban Sawma entered the church of Peter and Paul, since the residence of the throne of the lord pope is in it.[113] After the lord pope's passing away, the throne was entrusted to twelve men, called cardinals.[114] They were holding council to elect a pope, when Rabban Sawma had this message delivered to them: "We are ambassadors of King Arghun and of the *catholicos* of the East." Then the cardinals ordered them to enter. The Frank who had traveled with Rabban Sawma[115] had taught them that, when entering the residence of the lord pope, there was an altar before which they were to bow

---

111. This is not a consistent custom of medieval western European warfare. The more usual practice, for both western Europeans and Mongols, included attacking civilian bystanders.

112. Pope Honorius IV had died on April 3, 1287.

113. This is Old Saint Peter's Basilica, built by Constantine in the 300s and demolished in the early 1500s to be replaced by the new Saint Peter's Basilica, which is standing today. It was dedicated to Peter alone, not "Peter and Paul" as Rabban Sawma reports. At the time, it was not the residence of the popes (who lived in the Lateran palace, mentioned below), but it was the cathedral church (literally the "church of the throne") of the popes.

114. There were actually sixteen cardinals when Honorius IV died, although six of them died before his successor was elected the following year. The number twelve may have been chosen for symbolic reasons. The "council to elect a pope" was the papal conclave, a meeting of the cardinals behind locked doors to ensure the confidentiality of the deliberations.

115. Rabban Sawma's embassy included a Genoese ambassador from Arghun, who was named Tommaso Anfossi.

down and from there proceed to greet the cardinals. This is what they did, which pleased the cardinals. When Rabban Sawma arrived among them, no one rose before him: it was not the custom of those twelve men to do so, due to the honor of the papal throne. But they invited Rabban Sawma to sit with them, and one of them asked him, "How are you after such a difficult journey?" He replied, "By your prayers I am refreshed and rested!" He said to him, "What brings you here?" He replied to him, "The Mongols and the *catholicos* of the East sent me to the lord pope on account of Jerusalem, and they sent letters with me." The cardinals told him, "Rest for now; we will discuss this together later on." They assigned a residence to him, to which he was escorted.

After three days the cardinals sent for him. When he arrived before them, they began to question him: "What part of the world are you from, and why have you come?" And he gave the same answer. They asked him, "Where does the *catholicos* reside? And which of the apostles brought Christianity to your land?" He replied to them, "Saint Thomas, Saint Addai, and Saint Mari brought Christianity to our land, and to this day we follow the rules they gave us."[116] They asked him, "Where is the throne of the *catholicos*?" He answered them, "In Baghdad." They asked, "What is your office there?" He replied, "I am a minister in the patriarch's residence, chief of the disciples, and general overseer."[117] They said, "It is surprising that you, a Christian, a minister from the patriarchal throne of the East, have come as an envoy of the Mongol king!" He said, "Fathers, be aware that many of our own fathers went to the lands

116. Thomas was one of the original twelve apostles, who was credited in Syriac tradition with sending his follower Addai to Edessa (today Şanlıurfa in eastern Turkey), from which Addai sent Mari to what is today Iraq.

117. Rabban Sawma describes his role using three titles. The first one (*mshamshānā*) is often translated "deacon," but it may mean "minister or attendant" more generally. The second title (*rabbā d-talmīdē*) may suggest that Rabban Sawma was responsible for training new monks, or it may instead be a way of saying "foremost of the disciples [of the *catholicos*]," subordinating himself to this former student who now outranks him. The third title is "general overseer" (*sāʿōrā gāwānāyā*), his technical ecclesiastical office.

of the Mongols, the Turks, and the Chinese and converted them, so that today there are many Christians among the Mongols. There are even sons of kings and queens who have been baptized and confess Christ, and there are churches in their encampment. Christians are greatly honored, and many of the Mongols are believers. Therefore, the king, who is bound by affection to the lord *catholicos* and wishes to conquer Palestine and the lands of Syria, requests your help for the capture of Jerusalem. This is why he chose me and sent me: since I am Christian, my word will be believed by you." They asked him, "What is your confession, and what religion do you follow, that which the lord pope now accepts or another?" He replied, "No one has come to us easterners from the pope; the holy apostles I have named converted us, and to this day we follow what they handed down to us." They said to him, "What do you believe? Explain your creed."

Rabban Sawma's Creed, Which the Cardinals Requested from Him

Rabban Sawma replied to them, "I believe in one God, hidden, eternal, without beginning or end, Father, Son, and Holy Spirit, three identical, unseparated *qnōmē*.[118] There is no first or last among them, neither young nor old; they are one in nature but three as *qnōmē*: the Father is the begetter, the Son is the begotten, and the Spirit proceeds. I believe that one of the *qnōmē* of the royal Trinity, the Son, at the end of the ages[119] clothed himself with a perfect man, Jesus Christ, from the Holy Virgin Mary, was united to him personally, and in him saved the worlds; in his divinity he is eternally begotten by the Father and in his humanity

118. This is a technical Syriac term that roughly corresponds to hypostasis in Aristotelian philosophy. The Church of the East uses the term to refer to the three "Persons" of the Trinity, and also to the two "instantiated natures" of the incarnate Christ.

119. Cf. 1 Peter 1:20.

begotten within time by Mary. This unity is undivided and unbroken for eternity; the unity is without mixture, confusion, or composition. This unified Son is perfect God and a perfect man, two natures and two *qnōmē*, one person."

They questioned him, "Does the Holy Spirit proceed from the Father, or from the Son, or are they separate?" He replied, "Do the Father, the Son, and the Spirit share the same nature, or are they separate?" They replied, "They share the same nature but are separate in their individual characteristics." Rabban Sawma asked, "What are their individual characteristics?" They said, "Of the Father, begetting; of the Son, being begotten; of the Spirit, procession." He said, "Which of them is the cause of another?" They said, "The Father is the cause of the Son, and the Son is the cause of the Spirit." He said, "If they are equal in nature, in operation, in power, and in authority, and there are three *qnōmē* and no more, how can one be the cause of another? Necessarily the Spirit should also be the cause of something else, and the idea departs [from church teaching] to the confession of pagan sages.[120] We also find no demonstration that resembles this idea of yours: in fact, the soul is the cause of reason and of life, while reason is not the cause of life. The sphere of the sun is the cause of rays and heat, but the heat is not the cause of the rays. Therefore, we believe that it is better that the Father is the cause of the Son and the Spirit, and both were caused by him. Adam similarly fathered Seth and caused Eve to proceed: they are three individuals with respect to procreation and procession, but not distinct in their humanity in anything." The cardinals said, "We confess that the Spirit proceeds from the Father and the Son, but not in the way we have said. We tested you with argumentation."[121] He then said, "It is not right that two, three, or four causes exist for one thing; I think this is not in

120. Rabban Sawma may be comparing the progression of caused divine persons, which he thinks is implied by the view put forward by the cardinals, with the theory of emanations advanced by Neoplatonist philosophers such as Plotinus.

121. I.e., their earlier presentation that the Spirit proceeds from the Son alone was deliberately false to test how well he could argue.

conformity with our confession." They rejected his reasoning with various arguments, but they honored him for his reasoning.

He then said to them, "I have not come from distant lands to dispute, nor to make known matters of faith, but to receive the blessing of the lord pope and the temples of the saints, and to make known the message of the king and the *catholicos*. Now if you please, let us leave this discussion and you may keep yourselves secure,[122] and by commanding someone to show me the churches that are here and the shrines of the saints, you will do your servant and disciple a great favor." They then summoned the governor of the city and some monks, and commanded them to show him the churches and the places of the saints that are there. They accordingly left together and saw the places we shall now mention.

Rabban Sawma Visits Rome

First, they went to the church of Peter and Paul:[123] under the throne there is a chapel, where the body of Saint Peter was laid to rest, and above the throne is an altar. The altar sitting in the middle of that vast temple has four gates, each with double shutters of wrought iron. On that altar the lord pope celebrates Mass, and no one except him stands on the platform of that altar. They then saw the Chair of Saint Peter, upon which the lord pope is seated when they ordain him, and they also saw the cloth of pure cotton onto which our Lord imprinted his image to send it to King Abgar of Edessa.[124] The majesty of that temple and its

---

122. This may be referring to the cardinals returning to their conclave.

123. This is again Old Saint Peter's Basilica.

124. This is a story in Syriac tradition, not found in the Bible, that the king of Edessa (today in Turkey) sent a messenger and a painter to Jesus in Jerusalem, and Jesus, being unpaintable, imprinted his own image on the cloth and sent it to the king. The relic described here is probably the Veil of Veronica, which according to Latin tradition, also not found in the Bible, was a cloth used to wipe Jesus's face while he was carrying the cross to Calvary, and an image of his face was imprinted on the cloth, which he gave to Saint Veronica, a widow of Jerusalem.

magnificence cannot be described; it rests on 108 columns, and inside it is another altar, on which their king of kings receives his investiture and is proclaimed *empereur*,[125] that is, king of kings, by the pope. They say that after praying the pope takes the crown with his feet and makes him wear it, that is, he places it on his head, they say, to ensure that priesthood rules over kingship.[126]

Having visited all the churches and monasteries in great Rome, they went outside the city to the church of Saint Paul the Apostle,[127] whose tomb is also beneath the altar. Inside it is also the chain with which Paul was bound when they took him there. A gold reliquary was placed inside the altar, containing the head of Saint Stephen the martyr and the hand of Saint Ananias, who baptized Paul.[128] The staff of Saint Paul the Apostle is also there. Then they went to the place where he was crowned in martyrdom. They say that when his head was cut off, it bounced three times and each time cried "Christ, Christ"; from the three spots where it fell, waters gushed out, which are useful for healing and for giving help to everyone afflicted. There is a great chapel at the site,[129] in which the bones of martyrs and illustrious fathers are preserved; Rabban Sawma and his companions received a blessing there. They then went to the

125. The Syriac text reflects the French form of the word "emperor." This refers to "Holy Roman Emperor," a title that originated when Charlemagne was crowned by the pope in 800 CE, and in this period the Holy Roman emperors were German rulers crowned by the pope.

126. It was not customary for the pope to crown the emperor *with his feet*, and Rabban Sawma did not witness any coronation, so he is reporting what some informant told him. A story about Pope Celestine III (r. 1191–98) crowning Emperor Henry VI (r. 1191–97) in this manner was reported by Roger of Howden (d. 1202) and Ranulph Higden (d. 1363 or 1364), but it is unclear how Rabban Sawma heard the story. Roger Howden, *Chronica Magistri Rogeri de Houedene*, ed. William Stubbs (London: Longman, 1870), 3:102; Roger Howden, *The Annals of Roger de Hoveden*, trans. Henry T. Riley (London: H. G. Bohn, 1853), 2:197; Ranulph Higden, *Polychronicon Ranulphi Higden Monachi Cestrensis*, ed. Joseph R. Lumby (London: Longman, 1882), 8:100–101.

127. This is the church of Saint Paul Outside the Walls.

128. Cf. Acts 7:59–8:1 and 9:10–19.

129. This is the church San Paolo alle Tre Fontane.

church of Saint Mary and that of Saint John the Baptist,[130] where they saw the robe of our Lord, the seamless one.[131] In this church there is the board on which our Lord consecrated the offering and gave it to his disciples.[132] Upon it, every year, the pope celebrates the sacrament of Passover.[133] In the church there are also four bronze columns, each six cubits wide; they say they were brought from Jerusalem by the kings. There they saw the font of black polished stone in which Constantine, the victorious king, was baptized. In the temple there are 140 columns of white marble: indeed, the church is massive and broad. They saw the place of the disputation between Simon Cephas and Simon Magus, where the latter fell and broke his bones.[134] From there they went to the church of Saint Mary,[135] where a beryl reliquary was taken out for them, containing Saint Mary's robe and the wooden board on which our Lord slept as a child. In a silver reliquary they also saw the head of Matthias the Apostle, then again the foot of Philip the Apostle and the arm of James, the son of Zebedee, in the Church of the Apostles, which is there.[136] After this, they saw buildings that words cannot describe, and their stories of the buildings would make too long what is to be described; therefore we shall omit it.

Afterward Rabban Sawma and his companions returned before the cardinals, thanking them for having considered him worthy of visiting those shrines and receiving blessings there. Rabban Sawma requested

130. The church of Saint John the Baptist is Saint John Lateran. That of Saint Mary is described below.

131. Cf. John 19:23.

132. I.e., the Last Supper. Cf. Matthew 26:26–29.

133. Passover is what the Church of the East calls the Thursday before Easter, based on the interpretation that Jesus's Last Supper was a Passover meal. On that day the pope consecrates the Eucharist in this church.

134. The story of the apostle Peter (Simon Cephas) engaging in a miracle contest with Simon Magus is part of early Christian tradition. This is the church of Santa Francesca Romana.

135. This is the church of Santa Maria Maggiore.

136. This is the church of Santi Apostoli.

their permission to go to the kings beyond Rome. The cardinals permitted him to go but said, "We cannot give you a response until a pope is elected."

Rabban Sawma Travels to France or Frangistan[137]

From there they traveled to the land of Tuscany, where they were honored, and from there they went to Genoa. In that place there is no king: the people choose a great man to govern them, whoever they like.[138] When they learned that an envoy had arrived from King Arghun, their leader came out with all the people and brought them into the city with honor. There is a great church, dedicated to the holy San Lorenzo;[139] the blessed body of Saint John the Baptist is preserved there, in a pure silver reliquary. They also saw a six-sided emerald platter,[140] and the locals said to them, "In it our Lord ate the Passover with his disciples. It was brought when Jerusalem was captured."[141]

From there they went to the land of Lombardy;[142] they saw that the people there did not fast on the first Saturday of Lent. When they asked them, "Why are you doing this, and separating yourselves from all other Christians?" they replied, "This is our custom. When we first became

137. The former name reflects the French pronunciation; Frangistan is the Persian name for "land of the Franks."

138. At this time of Rabban Sawma's visit, Genoa was governed by two "captains of the people," Oberto Spinola and Oberto Doria.

139. I.e., Saint Lawrence. The Syriac text reflects the Italian pronunciation.

140. This is the Sacro Catino, which is green but not in fact made of emerald.

141. This refers to the First Crusade, which captured Jerusalem in 1099 and looted the holy city for relics.

142. Medieval Middle Eastern geographical texts used "Lombardy" to refer generally to northern Italy.

Christian, our fathers were weak in faith, and they could not fast: therefore their missionaries ordered them to fast for forty days."[143]

Rabban Sawma in France, or Frangistan

They later came to the place called Paris, before King Francis,[144] who sent many people out to meet them, and they brought them into the city with honor and great pomp. His lands extend for a distance of a month or more. King Francis appointed a place for them, and three days later he sent one of his emirs[145] to summon Rabban Sawma. When he arrived, the king rose before him and honored him, asking him, "Why have you come, and who sent you?" Rabban Sawma said to him, "King Arghun and the *catholicos* of the East sent me on account of Jerusalem." He made known to him all the words that he knew,[146] and gave him the letters that were with him and the gifts, that is, the presents he had brought. King Francis replied, "If the Mongols, who are not Christian, are fighting the Muslims to capture Jerusalem, we should fight even more. We shall come out with an army, Lord willing!" Rabban Sawma said to him, "Now that we have seen the glory of your kingdom and gazed upon the excellence of your strength with the eyes of flesh, we ask you to command the people of the city to show us the churches, shrines, and relics of saints, and all that is found here and not elsewhere, so that upon our return we may describe what we saw here and let it be known

143. In northern Italy, following the Ambrosian Rite, Christians do not fast on Saturdays during Lent. The explanation given here, however, does not match the Ambrosian Rite and may have been invented by Rabban Sawma or the author of the Syriac text.

144. The king of France at this time was Philip IV "the Fair" (r. 1285–1314). Perhaps the Syriac text reflects the French adjective *français*, and he was described to Rabban Sawma as "the French king."

145. Presumably a knight, but the text uses the Arabic term for a military commander.

146. This refers to the verbal message that was to be delivered alongside the written letters.

The royal basilica of Saint-Denis in Paris, which Rabban Sawma visited, included this giant rose window, almost forty feet across, in the north wing of the sanctuary.

in our lands." Then the king commanded his emirs, "Go and show them all the wonders with us, and afterward I will personally show them what I have with me." So, the emirs left with them.

They remained for over a month in that great city, Paris, and they saw all that is in it. There are 30,000 students, who learn both church teachings and secular teaching: the interpretation and commentaries of all the holy scriptures, and wisdom, that is, philosophy and logic, with medicine, geometry, arithmetic, and the science of planets and stars.[147] They are constantly writing and receive a salary from the king. They also saw, in a great church[148] there, the coffins where the dead kings are buried; on the tombs are their figures in gold and silver. Five hundred monks provide service to the royal burial site, whose food and drink is paid for by the king; they continue in fasting and prayer beside the royal tombs. On

147. This describes the University of Paris.

148. This is the church of Saint-Denis outside of Paris.

Edward I of England kneels in front of Philip IV of France to take an oath of loyalty on a Bible, as depicted in a fifteenth-century painting. As dukes of Aquitaine in southwestern France, the kings of England were also vassals required to swear loyalty to the kings of France as their liege lords.

the tombs are the crowns and weapons of those kings, along with their clothing. In short, they saw all that was glorious and honorable.

Afterward the king sent and summoned them, and they went to meet him in the church.[149] They saw him standing by the altar and greeted him. He asked Rabban Sawma, "Have you seen what we have? Is there anything else?" He thanked him. At once he ascended with the king to a golden upper room. The king opened it and brought out a beryl reliquary containing the crown of thorns that the Jews put on the head of our Lord when they crucified him.[150] So transparent was the beryl that

149. This is Sainte-Chapelle in Paris, built by Louis IX to house the Crown of Thorns, which he had acquired from the Latin emperor of Constantinople in 1238. The Crown of Thorns had been one of the relics in the Byzantine capital, which was captured by Latin crusaders during the Fourth Crusade in 1204.

150. Cf. Matthew 27:27–29. Notice the biblical account specifies that Romans, not Jews, put the crown of thorns on Jesus's head.

the crown could be seen in the reliquary without opening it. There was also a fragment of wood from the Cross. The king told them, "When our ancestors took Constantinople and looted Jerusalem, they took back these blessings." We blessed the king and begged him to give us a command to return. He told us, "I will send with you one of the greatest emirs who are by my side to give my reply to King Arghun."[151] He gave him presents and fine robes.

Rabban Sawma Before the King of *Angleterre*

They left there, that is, Paris, and went to the king of *Angleterre*,[152] in Gascony. When, after twenty days, they reached their city,[153] the people of the city came out to meet them and asked who they were. They replied, "We are envoys and we have come from beyond the eastern seas. We are ambassadors of the king and of the patriarch, and of the Mongol kings." People ran quickly to inform that king, who received them with joy and they brought them in to him. Immediately the members of Rabban Sawma's embassy gave to him King Arghun's command and the gifts he had sent, along with a letter from the lord *catholicos*. The king rejoiced greatly, especially when the conversation was on account of Jerusalem. His joy increased and he said, "We kings of these cities wear the cross as a sign on our person,[154] and we have no other thought than this. My resolve is strengthened when I hear that King Arghun is of the same mind!" He ordered Rabban Sawma to celebrate the Eucharist,

151. Philip sent the knight Gobert of Helleville as his ambassador to Arghun.

152. I.e., England (given in its French form). The king of England at this time was Edward I Longshanks (r. 1272–1307), who had already gone on crusade once, in 1271–72. Gascony, in southern France, was held by Edward as a fief from the king of France.

153. Bordeaux.

154. This refers to the practice of crusaders wearing a red cross on white fabric over their armor.

and he celebrated the glorious mysteries while the king and his court were standing; the king received the consecration.[155] That day the king gave a great banquet. Then Rabban Sawma said, "We ask, king, that you command for them to show us whatever is in this place of churches and shrines, so that we can report it when we return to the people of the East." He replied, "You will be able to tell King Arghun and all the people of the East that you saw the most amazing thing: that in the lands of the Franks there are not two confessions but only one, the one that confesses Jesus Christ, and everybody is Christian."[156] And he gave us many presents and money for the expenses.

Rabban Sawma Returns to Rome

From there we went to spend the winter in the city of Genoa. When we arrived there, we saw once again that it resembled the garden of paradise: its winter is not cold, and its summer is not hot. Green is found in it all year round, and there are trees whose leaves never fall off and which are never without fruit. A sort of vine grows there that bears grapes seven times a year, but no wine is made from it.

At the end of winter there came from the land of the Germans an important man, the lord pope's legate,[157] on his way to Rome. When he heard that Rabban Sawma was there, he went to greet him. As he arrived, they exchanged greetings and kissed each other in the love of Christ.[158] He told Rabban Sawma, "I have come to see you because I

---

155. Rabban Sawma, as a priest, can celebrate the liturgy and consecrate the Eucharist. Edward I received communion from him.

156. This is not true of western Europe as a whole, since there were Jewish populations, but it may be a misinterpretation of what Edward said if he referred to Gascony itself, from which he had just ordered the Jews to be expelled in 1287.

157. A legate is a church official sent by the pope to represent him for a particular mission. This legate was Cardinal Giovanni Boccamazza (d. 1309).

158. Cf. Romans 16:16.

heard you are a good and wise man, and also because you wish to go to Rome." Rabban Sawma said to him, "What can I say, my dear and honored friend? I have come on an embassy to the lord pope from King Arghun and the *catholicos* of the East, concerning Jerusalem. A year has passed, and a pope has not been seated in office. What should I go say or answer to the Mongols? Their heart is harder than flint, yet they are hoping to conquer the holy city, while those whose duty it would be do not even consider doing it or think anything of it. What we might go and say, we really do not know!" The legate told him, "What you're saying is true! I will go myself and make known your words, exactly, to the cardinals, and I will force them to elect a pope."

The legate left and arrived in Rome; he informed the council, who had elected a new pope.[159] On the same day, he sent a messenger to summon Rabban Sawma's embassy.

With the arrival of the messenger, they instantly left in the direction of Rome, where they arrived after fifteen days. When they asked who the newly elected pope was, they were told, "It is the bishop who spoke with you when you came the first time, and his name is Nicholas."[160] They were very glad. When they arrived, the lord pope sent people out to welcome them, an archbishop with many people. Rabban Sawma immediately went before the lord pope, who was seated on his throne. He bowed as he approached the pope, kissed his feet and hands, then retraced his steps backward with his hands joined together, and he said to the lord pope, "May your throne be established forever, our father, and may it be blessed above all the kings and peoples! May peace reign in the entire church during your days, to the ends of the earth![161] Now that I have

159. The election of a new pope had been delayed by several cardinals dying of illness and the others leaving the city of Rome for health reasons.

160. Girolamo Masci took the name Nicholas IV when he was elected pope and was in office 1288–92. He was earlier the bishop of Palestrina, and he was the first Franciscan to become pope.

161. Notice that Rabban Sawma articulates a very positive blessing for the pope, which nevertheless says nothing about papal claims of supreme authority over the entire church.

seen your face, my eyes have brightened, since I have not returned home brokenhearted. I thank God, who has considered me worthy of seeing you!" He gave him the gift from King Arghun along with his letters, and the gift from Mar Yahballaha the *catholicos*, that is, a blessing, and his letters. The lord pope rejoiced and was glad, and he honored Rabban Sawma more than was customary. He told him, "It will be good if you celebrate the feast with us, so you can see our custom." That day, in fact, was halfway through the Lord's Fast.[162] He replied, "Your command is high and exalted." The lord pope assigned a dwelling to him for his stay and appointed servants to give him everything he needed.

After a few days Rabban Sawma told the lord pope, "I would like to consecrate a Eucharist, so you too can see our custom." He was allowed to consecrate a Eucharist as he requested. That day a large crowd gathered, to see how the Mongols' ambassador consecrated a Eucharist. When they watched, they were glad and said, "The language is different, but the rite is the same!"[163] The day when he consecrated was the Sunday of the hymn *aynāw āsyā* [March 14, 1288].[164] After performing the sacraments, he went in before the lord pope and greeted him; the pope said to Rabban Sawma, "May God accept your offering and bless you, and may he forgive your trespasses and your sins!" Rabban Sawma replied, "With the forgiveness of trespasses and sins which I received from you, our father, I request from you, holy father, to receive communion from your hands, so that I may have complete pardon." The pope said, "It will be so."

On the following Sunday, which was Palm Sunday [March 21, 1288], thousands and tens of thousands without number gathered from dawn before the papal throne. They brought olive branches that the pope

162. I.e., the middle of Lent.

163. Since no one present could understand the Syriac language of Rabban Sawma's liturgy, "the rite" refers to the sequence of motions that accompanied consecrating the Eucharist (such as holding up the elements, breaking the bread, kneeling), but Rabban Sawma's motions could be called "the same" as the Roman rite only with a generous stretch of imagination.

164. This hymn was used on the Sunday before Palm Sunday in Lent.

blessed; he gave them in order to the cardinals, archbishops, bishops, emirs, and great men, and he was throwing them to the people. He arose from his seat and in great pomp they led him to the church, where he entered the sacristy and changed his clothes.[165] He put on red vestments woven with gold, gems, jacinths, and pearls, down to the sandals of his feet, that is, his shoes. He entered to the altar, walked out to the *bēma*,[166] and preached, exhorting the people. He consecrated the sacraments and gave the Eucharist first to Rabban Sawma, after the latter had confessed his sins. He forgave his trespasses and his sins, as well as those of his ancestors. He rejoiced greatly at receiving the Eucharist from the hand of the lord pope, and he took it while crying and weeping, giving thanks to God and thinking of the mercy poured out upon him.

Later, on the day of the holy Passover [March 25, 1288],[167] the lord pope went to the church of Saint John the Baptist,[168] after a great crowd had gathered, and he ascended to a large platform there, all decorated and ornate. Facing the platform is a large open space. The cardinals, archbishops, and bishops went in with him and began to pray. When they finished, the pope preached and exhorted the people, as was customary; not a sound was heard from the multitudes of people,[169] save for the "Amen," and when they said "Amen," the earth was shaken by the roar of their voices. From there he descended to face the altar and consecrated the oil of *myron*, that is, the oil of anointing.[170] Then he consecrated the atoning sacraments and gave them to the people. Then he left and went

---

165. The sacristy was a side room in which the special vestments for the liturgy were stored.

166. The *bēma* (or *ambo* in Latin) was a platform from which clergy read the Bible or preached to the congregation.

167. This is not the Jewish Passover, but instead how the Church of the East referred to the Thursday before Easter.

168. This is the church of Saint John Lateran.

169. Or this could mean "the sound of the pope's voice was not heard because of the multitude of the people."

170. This is chrism, a special consecrated oil used in church rituals.

to a great chapel,[171] where he gave to each of the reverend fathers two gold leaves and thirty silver sheets,[172] then he went out again. The lord pope gathered the people of his residence and washed their feet,[173] then patted them dry with a cloth tied around his loins, down to the last man. Once the Passover ritual was completed, halfway through the day, he gave a great banquet. Servants put before everyone his portion of the food; there were two thousand guests, more or less. When they took the bread away from the table, there were three hours left in the day.[174]

On the following day, which was that of the suffering of our Redeemer [March 26, 1288],[175] the lord pope put on a black mantle, as did all the bishops; they went out barefooted and walked to the church of the venerable Holy Cross.[176] The pope bowed down and kissed the cross, then he passed it on to each one of the bishops. When the crowds saw it, they uncovered their heads, kneeled down, and bowed down to it. The pope preached and exhorted the people. After making the sign of the cross to the four directions, when the prayer ended, he had part of the Passover offering brought and put the wine with it.[177] Only the lord pope received some of this offering, because it is not customary for Christians to make the offering on the day of our Redeemer's suffering, and he went back to his residence.

On the day called Saturday of Light [March 27, 1288], the pope went back to the church,[178] and they read the books of the Prophets

---

171. The chapel of Saint Lawrence in the Lateran palace.

172. This odd language seems to be describing Roman coins, in the custom of paying the clergy of Rome.

173. This is a ceremony particular to Maundy Thursday, imitating John 13:3–17.

174. I.e., midafternoon, implying that the feast (which started at noon) had lasted for three hours.

175. I.e., Good Friday.

176. This is the church of Santa Croce in Gerusalemme (in Rome).

177. On Good Friday, they did not consecrate a Eucharist in the normal way; in Rome they kept some bread from Thursday's mass (what the text calls "the Passover offering") and mixed it with wine to consecrate it, a process called *immixtio*.

178. Saint John Lateran again. This service is the Easter Vigil.

and the prophecies concerning Christ. They set up a font and over it they placed myrtle sprigs; the lord pope personally consecrated the water, baptized three children, and signed them with the sign of the cross. Then he went into the sacristy and changed from the vestments of the suffering into (other) liturgical vestments, whose value is incalculable; and he consecrated the sacraments.

On Resurrection Sunday [March 28, 1288],[179] the lord pope entered the holy church of Saint Mary. They gave the peace to each other, he and the cardinals, the archbishops, the bishops, and the congregation, and they kissed each other on the mouth.[180] The pope made the sacraments, and they received the Eucharist. He went back to his residence and gave a great feast, with endless joy.

On New Sunday [April 4, 1288],[181] the lord pope performed an ordination and ordained three bishops. Rabban Sawma's group witnessed their custom and celebrated the blessed festivals with them.

Once the festival was over, Rabban Sawma requested from the lord pope permission to return, but the latter said, "We want you to stay with us; you shall remain with us and we shall keep you like the apple of our eye." But Rabban Sawma replied, "Our father, I have come to serve you as an ambassador. If I had come at my own initiative, I would spend each day in this pointless life at the outer gate of your residence in your service. But when I go back, I will let the kings there know the good things you have lavished on my weakness. I think this will give great pleasure to the Christians. But I beg your holiness to give me as alms something of the relics that are here with you." The lord pope said, "If it were our custom to give anybody these relics, even if they were like mountains, among the tens of thousands of pilgrims they would have run out. But

179. I.e., Easter. The church is Santa Maria Maggiore.

180. Cf. Romans 16:16.

181. "New Sunday" is the Eastern Syriac name for the Sunday after Easter. John Romano has identified one of the bishops consecrated on this occasion as Matthew de Crambeth, the new bishop of Dunkeld in Scotland. John F. Romano, "The Travelogue of Rabban Sauma as a Source for Thirteenth-Century Liturgy," *Archiv für Liturgie-wissenschaft* 58/59 (2016/17): 94.

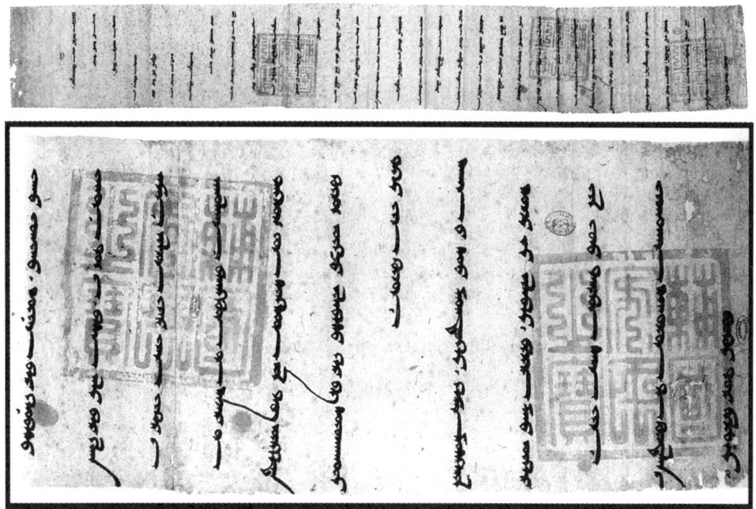

Part of Arghun's letter to Philip IV of France in 1289. This letter refers to Rabban Sawma's voyage of the preceding year.

since you came from a distant land, we will give you a little." He then gave him a small piece of our Lord Christ's robe, and of the *phakialion*,[182] that is, the cloak, of Saint Mary and other small relics of the saints there. He sent to Mar Yahballaha the *catholicos* one of his crowns, of pure gold, adorned with precious stones, red and gold-embroidered fabrics for liturgical vestments, shoes encrusted with tiny pearls, sandals, also a ring he took from his own finger, and an open letter, namely, that in him was collected the patriarchal authority over all the eastern peoples.[183] To

182. This is a Greek term, used in Syriac to describe a special type of cloak worn by Eastern Syriac bishops, but in this text referring to the mantle of Jesus's mother.

183. As is made clear from the letter itself, which survives, the pope saw this letter as exercising his universal jurisdiction to invest a subordinate patriarch with authority, and scholars have interpreted this episode as Rabban Sawma and Mar Yahballaha recognizing papal authority. The Syriac is more ambiguous, however, and might instead describe their view that the pope recognized Mar Yahballaha as a fellow patriarch, over "the East" as the pope is over "the West" (cf. the following section heading, though that is likely not from Rabban Sawma, being instead from the Syriac author).

Rabban Sawma himself he gave an open letter of overseership over all Christians, and he blessed him. He took upon himself the expenses of Rabban Sawma's journey, amounting to 1,500 *mithqal*s of red gold.[184] He sent to King Arghun something as a blessing. He embraced and kissed Rabban Sawma and sent him away. Rabban Sawma thanked our Lord, who had made him worthy of such good things.

Rabban Sawma's Return from Rome, and from the Lord Pope, the *Catholicos* Patriarch of Romania[185] and of All the Westerners

He returned, crossing the same sea he had come from, and arrived safely before King Arghun, with health of body and preservation of soul. He gave him the document of blessings along with the gifts he had brought from the lord pope, as well as from all the kings of the Franks. He made known how warmly they had welcomed him and that they had obeyed well the commands that he brought. He told them of the marvels he had seen and the might of the kings. King Arghun was happy and delighted by his report; he thanked him, saying, "We have made you work hard, when you are an old man! From now on we will not let you depart from us, but we will establish a church at our royal court, where you shall serve and pray." Rabban Sawma said, "If this is what my lord the king commands, let Mar Yahballaha the *catholicos* come here to receive the gifts sent to him by the lord pope, and the liturgical items that he has granted him, and let him establish and consecrate the church founded by the king at his royal court." These things happened in this way.

Since it is not our aim to repeat and arrange the various things Rabban Sawma did and the things he saw, we have omitted much of what he himself wrote in the Persian language, and the things mentioned

184. I.e., about fifteen pounds of pure gold.

185. I.e., the land of the Romans.

here have been added to or abridged, according to the purpose of the inquiry.

The Good Deeds of King Arghun and His Death

And so, in the Greek year 1599 [1288 CE], King Arghun ordered Mar Yahballaha to visit him in the camp, as Rabban Sawma had requested. For the honor of the *catholicos* and to give all the Christians who profess Christ new courage, and to increase their love for him, he established a church at the court of his throne, so close that the ropes of the church's tent crossed the ropes of his palace.[186] He gave a great banquet that lasted three days; King Arghun personally served food to the *catholicos* and handed the cup to him and to all the people in his service. The bishops, holy fathers, priests, deacons, and monks were occupied with night prayers and the church service. The king ensured that the church was not deprived of the sound of a clapper.[187] He thereby increased the glory of eastern and western Christians, until they were proclaiming with one voice, "Blessed be the Lord who enriched us! The Lord has visited his people and accomplished salvation for them!"[188]

When the camp moved, the priests moved the church along with all its contents. Rabban Sawma was the director of that church, the manager, and the steward of the salaries of the priests, deacons, administrators, and caretakers of that church. Indeed, King Arghun, from his great

186. Mongol yurts (or *gers*) did not use ropes, but ropes were used for the large pavilions constructed for special occasions. Such pavilions were massive, accommodating many hundreds of people. Even the "church's tent" was likely not small, enabling processions with candles inside and perhaps gathering a congregation of dozens of people.

187. Where western European Christians used bells, Christians in the Middle East used various kinds of wooden or metal "clappers," which make a loud noise when struck.

188. Luke 1:68.

affection for him, commanded that offerings for him and prayers for his welfare should never cease.

The following year, that is, the Greek year 1600, in the month of September [1289 CE], King Arghun visited the patriarchal residence in the city of Maragha to see the lord *catholicos*. In the month of August he had baptized his son,[189] and he commanded him to receive the atoning sacraments. In this way the proclamation of eternal life increased, and the gospel of the kingdom of heaven spread in the whole world, until people from every land, and not only Christians, gathered at the patriarchal residence to draw help from it, to have the lord *catholicos* intercede on their behalf to fulfill their needs.

But after the situation that we mentioned had been going on for a little while, God, the Lord of all, the Lord of death and departure, transported King Arghun to the garden of delights and Abraham's bosom.[190] The whole church under the sky mourned his departure, because in his time many things were reformed that had happened before his time and had been corrupted.

Who is not grieved by a transfer of kingship? How could it not be? It is a difficult situation for anybody, and a bitter one to describe, even when one knows the king's great men and all the members of the royal house, not to mention the kings of one's time!

King Geikhatu and Mar Yahballaha

The church found itself in this situation for some time; then suddenly the younger brother of the deceased king rose to power, named Irinjin Torji, who was crowned as King Geikhatu. He held the royal scepter and sat on his brother's throne. He became king in 1602

189. Arghun's son Öljeitü, the future Ilkhan, was baptized with the name Nicholas in 1289 in honor of Nicholas IV.

190. Cf. Luke 16:22.

of the Greek era, in the month of August in that year [1291].[191] The world was quiet, confusion fled and hid itself, the light of justice dawned and revealed itself, because the blessed King Geikhatu did not turn aside from the path of his fathers: he confirmed all the people of religion, each in his own office, and honored the leaders of all dogmas, whether Christians, Muslims, Jews, or pagans,[192] and he had no favoritism at all. Neither did he waffle or turn aside from justice, and gold was like dung in his eyes; his alms were limitless, his gifts endless. Whoever asked received from him, as is written,[193] and whoever sought found, as is well demonstrated by facts.

After he had begun to reign in the month of the year mentioned, on the day of the memorial of Saint Mary (may her prayers protect the world), which falls in the middle of the month of August [August 15, 1291], he entered the church founded by Doquz Khatun in the blessed camp.[194] They were then on the mountain called Ala Tagh. When our father the *catholicos* had made the sacraments, the king rejoiced greatly and was glad; he gave the *catholicos* a present of 20,000 *dīnārs* and nine robes of fine silk brocade. On that day, the sons of kings and the daughters of queens, the emirs, the great men, and the armies were all gathered there.

The glory of the holy catholic church[195] increased as at first or higher, and Christians found renewed courage and strength when they knew the attitude of the victorious king, heard his words, and held with their own hands his gifts and his favors. Day by day their glory increased,

---

191. Geikhatu became Ilkhan on July 23, 1291, after his brother Arghun died on March 30, 1291.

192. In the Ilkhan's court, this usually referred to Buddhists.

193. Cf. Matthew 7:8.

194. Doquz Khatun (d. 1265) was the chief wife of Hülegü, the founder of the Ilkhanid dynasty.

195. Notice the use of "holy catholic church" not to refer to the papacy but to the Church of the East. Medieval Christians outside of Europe used "catholic" not in opposition to "Protestant" but in the older meaning of "universal," which they understand to refer to their own churches.

and the honor of their church grew. All this was due to the great care and noble governance of the lord *catholicos*, and the manner of his discernment for how to flatter royal princes.

Rabban Sawma, because he was now old, was weary of the rough lifestyle of the Mongols and life in the open. So he sought an edict from the victorious King Geikhatu to build a church in the city of Maragha and to put in it the liturgical items of the church that the late King Arghun had established in the camp. His request was granted by the king; once he had obtained permission, he immediately left for Maragha with the liturgical items of the lord *catholicos*. He founded and built a beautiful church dedicated to Saint Mari and Saint George, the glorious martyr. Inside it were placed relics of the Forty Martyrs, of Saint Stephen, Saint James the Dismembered, and Saint Demetrios the martyr. He decorated it with fine things of the liturgy and secured the endowments necessary to supply all its needs, with the aid of the illustrious *catholicos* Mar Yahballaha. In the summer of the following year [1292 CE], the victorious King Geikhatu came to the patriarchal residence in Maragha twice and remained for three days with the lord *catholicos*. He rejoiced very greatly and presented lavish gifts to the lord *catholicos*: a gold *paiza*, that is, a tablet called *sunqur*,[196] and 7,000 *dīnār*s.

The Death of Rabban Sawma and of the Kings Geikhatu and Baidu

Rabban Sawma was working day and night in that church that he built and polishing the things. The total expenses that were for this church, the endowment, that is, the *waqf*, appointed for it, was about 105,000 *zūzē*.[197] Rabban Sawma was constantly busy with his service

196. The *paiza* was a tablet of authority granted by the Mongol ruler; a golden one decorated with a falcon (Mongolian *sunqur*) granted particular privileges.

197. *Waqf* is the Arabic term for endowments. The *zūzē* referred to were probably silver *dirhams*.

and his prayer, and he was insistent that the offering he had established in that church should be made continually. He had much rest in a cell beside the church that he had founded. Indeed, to this day he is its glory, and prayers and offerings are continual in it. May our Lord grant him as a wage for his labor the delights of the heavenly kingdom and a place with the saints in the highest heaven.

When he had completed the church that we mentioned, he went down to Baghdad to serve the lord *catholicos* in the Greek year 1605 [1293–94 CE]. In October of that year [1293], King Baidu, the son of King Abaqa's brother, gave a great banquet in honor of the *catholicos* in a place called Shahrazur, and he gathered to that company the people who supported his kingship.[198] Rabban Sawma rose from the feast with his constitution wrecked and he fell down, gripped by a fever. On the following day he left King Baidu and reached the town of Arbil, to settle urgent matters and for refreshment with members of the church. But Rabban Sawma's illness grew worse and he was suffering. He lasted until the *catholicos* reached the city of Baghdad; then his illness got worse, his health fled, and his hope to live was cut off. He left this world of vanity and torments for the holy world and the city of saints, the heavenly Jerusalem, on the night of the Sunday after Epiphany, whose responsive hymn is *l-ʿēdtāk luqdam*, on January 10 of that year [1294 CE]. His holy body was buried in the Court of the Romans,[199] north of the altar, outside, in the inner courtyard on the south side of the prayer hall. May his portion be with the *catholicos* fathers, among whom he is buried! May our Lord grant him rest and make him stand at his right on the great day of judgment,[200] when everyone will be repaid according to his deeds through the balance of justice and the scales of truth!

198. Baidu only became king in 1295, so the reference to him as a king here is an anachronism. Shahrazur is a region between Arbil and Hamadan.

199. This was the residence of the *catholicos* in Baghdad before the Mongol conquest of the city, and many patriarchs were buried there.

200. Cf. Matthew 25:31–46.

Mar Yahballaha the *catholicos* endured much misery at his passing away, and his cries rose to the sky. He led public lamentations, so that no one could say he was mourning privately. The great men, the powerful, the governors, and all the spiritual fathers in the city of Baghdad came to comfort him. After three days, he hardly accepted comforting, but he returned to his throne. It was right for him to grieve: the law of nature commanded it. The deceased was indeed brave, useful, a help in the court of the patriarchal residence, not only for the lord *catholicos* but for all the Christians who came to him.

After spending the winter in Baghdad, the *catholicos* left on the day of the great feast [April 18, 1294][201] for the [royal] camp. He met the victorious King Geikhatu at Ala Tagh, the royal camp. He honored him with numerous presents: the king gave him a prized fur and two splendid mules; he granted him a *sukur*, that is, a parasol, and presented him with 60,000 *zūzē*. In short, the king did not refuse anything that the *catholicos* opened his mouth and requested. Upon his return from the presence of the victorious king, he laid the foundations of the holy monastery of Saint John the Baptist, on the north side of the city of Maragha, at a distance of about a third of a *farsakh*.[202] That same year, at the end of the month of June, he almost completed the wall and the sanctuaries, up to the edge of the vault.

And suddenly storms burst and strengthened the waves of confusion in the kingdom. The emirs were disloyal to the king, tempests of sufferings raged across the world, and disturbance came down upon creation. Innocent people were massacred, and many villages were forcefully taken into captivity by the armies. In the winter of the year 1606 of the Greeks [1294–95 CE], with the roads between Azerbaijan, Baghdad, and Diyar Bakr cut off, contentious people never ceased from the contentions they stirred up, until they violently destroyed King Geikhatu and handed over the kingdom to King Baidu. This poor man even agreed, fearing for his life, and remained on the throne from

201. I.e., Easter.

202. A *farsakh* is about 3.5 miles long, so this is a bit over a mile.

April 24 to September 25 of that year [1295 CE], more or less. This one also ruled and reigned while troubled and prolonged his days while fearful. The tricks of those five months, the plots, and the ambushes that were between him and the victorious king Ghazan, son of the late King Arghun, and what the enemies schemed, this account cannot contain here, otherwise we would prolong the story, and the account that is desired would end up turning into something different. In short, the murderers of the blessed King Geikhatu also schemed to kill his successor, King Baidu. Division came and the inhabited world was disturbed; the Muslim people were stirred up to take revenge on the church and its members for the destruction that had come to them at the hands of the father of these kings.[203] And suddenly, on the Sunday of the hymn *lā mṣē pummā*, which fell on September 25 of that year [1295 CE], the news was heard that King Baidu had fled and perished. With it came such trials that it is truly abandonment by God.

The Persecution of Mar Yahballaha and the Christians of Maragha

An emir named Nawruz, a man without fear of God, was stirred up, and he sent letters by messengers and spread to the four corners of this kingdom's lands that churches should be destroyed, the altars should be overturned, the sacraments should cease, the chants and clappers should be blotted out, and the Christian leaders, along with the leaders of the Jewish synagogues and their great men, should be killed.

That same night the lord *catholicos* was held prisoner in his residence in Maragha; outside, nobody realized it until dawn. On the morning of that day, a Monday, they entered the residence and plundered everything that was in it, old or new, so that not a peg remained in a wall. In the night of the

---

203. "The father of these kings" is Hülegü, the founder of the Ilkhanate, who captured Baghdad and destroyed the Abbasid caliphate in 1258. Here the author asserts that the Muslims sought revenge for this destruction from Christians.

following Tuesday, September 27, the *catholicos* was tortured all night long by those who had seized him. Of the bishops who were with him, some they tied up naked; others had left behind their clothes and fled; others had jumped down from high places. They hanged the *catholicos* upside down and took a napkin, that is, a handkerchief, put ashes in it, and tied it over his mouth. One poked his chest with a skewer, saying, "Leave this faith of yours, so you will not die! Become a Hagarene[204] and you will be saved!" The patriarch wept and did not reply. They hit him with a staff on his thighs and buttocks, then led him up to the roof of the residence, saying, "Give us gold and we will leave you alone! Show us your treasures, make known to us what you have hidden, uncover what you have concealed, and we will spare you!"

The lord *catholicos*, because he was clothed in a weak body and subject to suffering, was afraid of death; he then began to cry out on the roof, "Where are my disciples? How could those I have brought up have run away? What use are our possessions? Come, ransom your father from these oppressive sellers! Redeem your leader!" The people, men, women, youths, and children wailed with bitter tears in the midnight darkness, but out of fear no one was able to approach. Instead, they sought help in tears and refuge in prayer, saying, "Mountains, fall on us . . . hills, cover us!"[205] The prediction of the prophet of the Syrians was fulfilled:[206]

Because we scorned the Way itself
And a great shame we made it,
He made us a shame to outsiders
That we might drink mocking from them . . .
Unclean men ruined our churches
In which we had not prayed properly,
And chopped up the altar before which
We had not served him worthily.

---

204. I.e., a Muslim.

205. Luke 23:30.

206. This is a way of referring to the poet Ephrem (d. 373). This portion is from his *Memre on Faith* (VI.379–82 and 465–68) and had been incorporated into the liturgy of the Church of the East.

In short, so that we do not prolong the story, one of the disciples from the patriarchal residence went and borrowed 15,000 *zūzē*, and he paid it a little at a time, hoping to free the *catholicos*. When those who had seized the *catholicos* had received the sum of 5,000 *dīnārs*, along with the liturgical cups, plates, and everything there was in the residence, along with the ransom, they went out from the residence that Tuesday at midday.

A large riot arose: the Muslim people hastily came to ruin the great church of the holy martyr Saint Shallita, and they ruined it. They carried off all that was in it, the curtains and liturgical items. The raging of their yelling and storm of their shouts very nearly shook the earth and its inhabitants.

Perhaps the reader of this story, who has not found himself in the middle of that storm, will think the writer is only making up tales, but what is true to say—and the one telling this calls God as a witness!—is that not even one of the things that happened can be spoken or written.

As for the church that Rabban Sawma had built, the Armenian king, Het'um *tagavor*,[207] had come to it, saving it from destruction with his many gifts and his troops. The *catholicos*, having escaped his kidnappers, fled to him and was hidden for that night. The following morning, Wednesday [September 28, 1295], there came an emir sent by Nawruz who was mentioned, and he brought an order for the execution of the *catholicos*. He said to many people, including the king *tagavor*, "Show me the *catholicos*, as I have something to say to him." As soon as he heard this, the lord *catholicos* trembled in his heart. He fled from there and left the *tagavor*. The king *tagavor* appeased the emir with some gifts that he gave him and left Maragha.

A few days later, the king *tagavor* also went to Tabriz.[208] The lord *catholicos*, in disguise, went out alone like one of his servants[209] and

207. *Tagavor* is the Armenian word for "king." Het'um II (d. 1307) reigned intermittently in Cilicia from 1289 until 1303.

208. Tabriz is a city in northwestern Iran that was the capital of the Ilkhanate at this time.

209. It is very unusual for someone as important as the *catholicos* to travel without a retinue of servants.

accompanied him to the city of Tabriz, because King Ghazan had arrived there. The *catholicos* was concealed for seven days, until the *tagavor* went before King Ghazan and informed him of the situation, and he required him to go see the king. Since the servants of the patriarchal residence were scattered, there remained with the lord *catholicos* a few poor children who followed him; they went to King Ghazan with him. The king did not know him, and when he greeted him, he asked him two things: "Where are you from? What is your name?" and nothing else. The *catholicos* replied and blessed him; then he left, though trembling had entered his bones. It was not only from fear of dying, but for the end to which the baptized Christians had come! And because the encouraging angel and his watchful mind exhorted him, "No trial has come upon you but that which is common to humanity,"[210] he was still encouraging himself with tears and laments, while saying:

> Oh, that my head were waters, and my eyes a fountain of tears,
> That I might weep day and night, for the breaking of the daughter of my people![211]

That is how things were. It was cold during those days, and the camp was moved to Mughan,[212] the winter campsite. The accursed Nawruz was in Tabriz. The *catholicos*, without money and without an animal to ride or a pack animal, returned to Maragha. He remained in his residence for a few days, and again other extortionists came,[213] but he took refuge in fleeing from their hands. With the great financial losses, he was moving around day by day.

---

210. 1 Corinthians 10:13.

211. Jeremiah 8:23.

212. This is a plain along the Aras River in modern Azerbaijan.

213. Just as earlier he was held for ransom, so again people show up demanding money from him. The same term is used for creditors and tax collectors, but he does not have debts to them, nor are they demanding regular taxes.

It is known that the end of all worldly glory leads its affair to humiliation from God, and that at the end of long humiliation for the sake of God, glory is joined with it.

When, during that winter, the *catholicos* sent one of his disciples to the camp to renew the decrees[214] and to explain the state of things, he too fled back: no one was receiving a message from Christians or feeling pity for the oppressed. The disciple barely managed to escape from the hands of an apostate who had abandoned his faith and become a Hagarene.

After the feast of Christmas in the Greek year 1607 [December 25, 1295], on the Sunday of the hymn *mārēkul kad badmutā* [January 1, 1296], messengers of the accursed Nawruz again descended upon the *catholicos*, carrying orders: "*Catholicos*, give us the 10,000 *dīnār*s which you received in the time of King Geikhatu; here is the *tamgha* (that is, the written document stamped with the emir's seal) for them to be returned!"

The patriarchal residence had been empty and worthless; the people of the residence, as soon as they heard this, had scattered, taking refuge in fleeing. The *catholicos* remained in the hands of those Hagarized[215] Mongols and of those who had summoned them. Fear fell on the people of the church. How much? If you would say how much, even the bishops who were in the residence fled, and only the lord *catholicos* remained in the hands of those cursed bullies. That night he promised to bestow a village upon them, but they would accept nothing but gold. As soon as they threatened him with beatings, he began to borrow money and bribe them. In the course of that Sunday, before night fell, they received 2,000 *dīnār*s.

Some of the disciples conspired with the lord *catholicos* to help him escape and deliver him from the hands of those people. He was afraid of this, but when they forced him, he obeyed. As the rooster crowed, they let him escape through a small window of the house in which he was

214. I.e., the decrees issued by each new ruler granting the *catholicos* certain privileges as leader of the Christians.

215. Just as "Hagarene" is a derogatory term for Muslims, so this is a derogatory reference to people who had become Muslim.

confined, so narrow that even when fully open, one would have thought that not even a child could come out of it. They lowered him to the ground, and he went and hid in other places. Those bullies, at sunrise, were confused and did not know what to do. They were also afraid that someone might demand vengeance for him, saying, "You killed him!" At that very time they left the city and went by the road to Baghdad.

They had just left when another messenger came, someone more evil than Nawruz of cursed life. With him was a Christian who had become a Hagarene, and he brought another order that 36,000 *dīnār*s should be given to him. Since the lord *catholicos* was in hiding, those oppressive messengers seized some disciples from the residence and made their bodies weak with many beatings and tortures. They hung them upside down outside on cold and snowy days, the worst that were ever seen. After the whole city had gathered to free them, they were barely rescued from the hands of those wicked men by paying 16,000 *dīnār*s. The *catholicos* and everyone with him, whether bishops, monks, or laypeople, continued to be persecuted by everyone, and they hid among the houses of laypeople, and when it became known that they were hiding in a certain house, they moved at once to another. This situation lasted until the great feast of the Resurrection [March 25, 1296].

King Ghazan Honors Mar Yahballaha

When the sun had descended into the sign of Aries [late March or early April] and creation had warmed up a little, the *catholicos* sent one of the monks from the residence to the victorious King Ghazan, to the place called Mughan, the Mongol rulers' winter location, to bless the king and let him know what had happened to him.

When that monk reached the camp and had diligently met all the emirs, they brought him into the victorious king, and he repeated exactly the words that the lord *catholicos* had said to him: "May your throne be blessed, king, and be stable forever, and may your descendants be confirmed upon it eternally!" The king asked, "Why did the *catholicos* himself

A gold *dīnār* minted by Ghazan in 1301.

not come to us?" The monk replied, "Because he is in a state of confusion, he was hanged upside down and beaten severely, and his head hit the ground. Because of the intense pain stirred up against him, he could not come to bow down to the king. For this reason, he sent me to bless you, my lord the king. When the victorious king comes in peace to Tabriz, the *catholicos*, whether healthy or ill, will come to greet him and bow down to him."

God made these words find mercy in the eyes of the king. He issued decrees for the *catholicos* according to custom: one, that the *jizya* would not be taken from Christians;[216] and that none of them should leave his confession;[217] and that the *catholicos* shall live according to his custom, be treated according to his rank, exercise authority upon his throne, and grasp the scepter of strength over his jurisdiction. He also issued a decree throughout the regions, explicitly addressing the emirs and troops, commanding them to return all that they had extorted from the *catholicos* or

216. The *jizya* was a tax instituted by early Muslim rulers to be taken from non-Muslim individuals. When the Mongols conquered the Middle East, they did not require the *jizya* of non-Muslims. As Mongol rulers converted to Islam, it was a question whether they would reinstitute the *jizya*, and there was some back-and-forth on the question.

217. I.e., this prohibits conversion from Christianity to any other religion.

his bishops, and those people of Baghdad and their messengers whom we mentioned above to return what they had taken. He also granted and gave 5,000 *dīnārs* for the *catholicos*'s expenses, while saying, "These will be the amount until he appears before us."

Because Christ does not desert his Church, he is the one who binds up the brokenhearted[218] and saves the humble in spirit. He is "a refuge for the poor and their helper in times of affliction."[219] Indeed, God disciplines with mercy and inflicts suffering to obtain:[220] his reproach teaches the discerning that he is not indifferent,[221] and will not allow one being tested to be tested beyond his strength. Then he turns to him in mercy, heals his wounds, and gathers him into the sheepfold of life, after testing him. Indeed, God (may his glory be worshipped) had turned the heart of the king toward his people:

> Like streams of water, so is his heart in the hand of the Lord;
> He turns it wherever he will.[222]

From that day on, rays of salvation began to shine upon the entire Church.

Around Arbil the churches had been damaged for a while; around Tabriz and Hamadan they were entirely blotted out, and their foundations had been pulled out of the ground. In Mosul and its province, and in Baghdad, the churches had been ransomed for high prices and tens of thousands of gold coins.[223] But the church built in Baghdad by the *catholicos* Makkika by order of the victorious King Hülegü and the

---

218. Cf. Psalm 147:3; Isaiah 61:1.

219. Psalm 9:9.

220. This phrase is terse and unclear in the Syriac original.

221. This is an allusion to Ephrem, *Sermones rogationum* III. See Thomas J. Lamy, ed., *Sancti Ephraem Syri Hymni et sermones* (Mechelen, Belgium: H. Dessain, 1889), 3:35–36. The line was also incorporated into church services.

222. Proverbs 21:1.

223. The text uses an archaic coin term, "darics," which does not seem to have been a specific denomination in the Mongol period.

Christian queen Doquz Khatun was taken, along with the residence and the palace that had belonged to the Arab kings.[224] When Hülegü, the ancestor of the present kings, had captured and subdued Baghdad, he had given the palace to the *catholicos* Mar Makkika, to establish prayers in it for him and his family forever. But it was not enough for those who seized this church to reclaim the patriarchal residence; they also forced the Christians to remove the bones of the two *catholicos* fathers who had been buried there,[225] along with the bishops, the monks, and the believers. These things were by order of that son of destruction, the cursed, execrable Nawruz, the hater of all justice, the enemy of truth, and the lover of lying.

When the monk returned to the lord *catholicos*, he brought the decree with him and made known the emirs' love and the great benevolence of the victorious king toward him. The gate of the patriarchal residence was opened, the *catholicos* sat on his throne, gathered the scattered disciples, and brought near the household members who had gone far away. That day the decrees were read aloud in the *dīwān*, that anyone who had taken something from the patriarch must return it. From that, the *catholicos* took the amount for going to King Ghazan. He left Maragha for the place called Ujan in the month of July of the Greek year 1607 [1296], which then fell in the month of Ramadan.[226]

Two days after his arrival, he went before the victorious king with the honor that was appropriate. The king had incense burned, according

224. "Arab kings" refers to the Abbasid caliphs who ruled Baghdad before Hülegü conquered it in 1258. Hülegü and his chief wife Doquz Khatun gave the palace to the *catholicos* Makkika II (d. 1265).

225. After Makkika II converted the Abbasid palace into a church and patriarchal residence, he and his successor Denha I (d. 1281) were buried inside of it, as were other Christians of various ranks. When Muslims repossessed the church, they would not want Christians' corpses buried within it.

226. Ujan is a town east of Tabriz, which was at this time the summer capital of the Ilkhanate. Ramadan is a month in the Islamic calendar. Because the Islamic calendar is strictly lunar, it shifts relative to the solar calendar, but in 1296 CE the month of Ramadan corresponded to July 3–August 1.

to custom; and seated him at his right. He had wine brought, and the king held the cup for the *catholicos* and also for all the bishops who accompanied him.[227] From then on he began to be fond of him, but however much the king increased his honor, even a little, so did hatred increase in the hearts of the enemies. They plotted evil schemes, and everything that was happening, they were sending to inform that son of destruction, the cursed Nawruz.

Looting and Murder in Maragha Again

In the Greek year 1608 [1296–97], the victorious king went down to spend the winter in Baghdad, and the lord *catholicos* stayed in Maragha.

It happened that a man entered Maragha who was called Shaykh El Temür,[228] who spread the news that he was carrying a decree that whoever did not abandon Christianity and renounce his confession would be killed. He then further worsened the situation by inventing new things that had never been heard before in this world. When the Muslim people heard this, they became enraged, strengthened, emboldened in heart, and hardened. With a rush the whole people arrived at the patriarchal residence and looted whatever they found. This happened on the Wednesday [March 6, 1297] after the Sunday of the hymn *tāw nāwdē wa-nshabbaḥ*, during the Lord's Fast.[229]

When the story came out that the bully had done this without a royal command, but out of his evil inclination and the force of his malice, the emirs and the powerful people in Maragha gathered and took counsel to give judgment on the following Sunday and bring back the precious

227. It was a major honor for the Mongol ruler to personally hold out the cup for someone else to drink.

228. Nothing else is known about this person; even his name is uncertain, since the Syriac text reads *Shenak Eltamur*.

229. I.e., the Wednesday after the second Sunday in Lent, according to the Eastern Syriac calendar.

things that those bullies had looted from the residence. They were items of great value, among which was the gold seal that the king of kings Möngke Qa'an[230] (may our Lord make his soul rest and grant him a place among the saints) had bestowed on the patriarchal residence, the crown that the lord pope had sent to the residence and another seal, of silver, that the late King Arghun had given the *catholicos*.

When the Muslim people gathered before the emirs and judges, and staffs were brought to punish the rioters and beat them, they all immediately began to shout in unison. They took stones in their hands, plugged their ears, and chased the emirs and powerful men, each one to his house. If a Christian fell into their hands, they hit him and wounded him without mercy.

In that rush they reached the patriarchal residence. They pulled down all the buildings, even to the beams of the ceilings. As for the monks who were in the residence and the children who had gone up onto the roof to hide themselves, they broke their heads with stones. One of the disciples from the residence, when he saw these things, turned back against them and hit some of them. They became even more infuriated, and one climbed up behind him and struck him with a sword, and he cut off his head and threw it down. The monks who were there threw themselves down, and some shattered their bones. One of the bullies, thirsty for the blood of Christians, and seeing them fling themselves down to escape, grabbed a knife and stabbed a monk to death. The others were carried away by some believers who sheltered them in their homes. The treasury that was in the holy church of Saint George, which was built by Rabban Sawma, was opened and everything that belonged to the residence—dishes of brass and iron, carpets, crates of produce, which had escaped the first looting—was taken and plundered at once. But in the looting of those people, the church escaped and was rescued from being pulled down and ruined. This was the ultimate aim of those bullies, but God, in his mercy for that church, delayed them when they looted it.

230. Möngke reigned 1251–59.

In short, this ending was worse than the previous looting, so much that the tongue cannot speak it, nor can the pen of the most capable scribe write it.

If God had not had mercy, and if the believing queen Boraqchin Egächi[231] had not been there to hide the *catholicos* and the bishops in her house, concealing them with the help of God who assisted, the church would have been reduced to lowering the head and covering the face, because the troublemakers were threatening murder.

Five days later they went to a place called Jaghatu,[232] and from there they moved to the mountain called Siyah Kuh, until the king returned from Baghdad to Hamadan. Near this city the *catholicos* went in before him. When he saw him, the king felt pained for him and for his misfortune. He issued a decree and sent a messenger, commanding that all the people of Maragha be captured, bound, and beaten until they gave back what they had looted from the patriarchal residence, and also that they should rebuild the churches as they were before. After much effort, and the beatings and tortures that were inflicted, they brought out a small part, but the rest remained.

Riots and Battles in the Citadel of Arbil

This misfortune that overtook the patriarchal residence was not sufficient, but the believers inside the citadel of Arbil fell into a misfortune greater than this. It happened because the people of the city, that is, the Muslims and the Kurds, wanted to demolish the church. It happened that some Christians from among the king's soldiers, who were

231. The "queen" who sheltered Mar Yahballaha was probably the same as Hülegü's concubine with the same name, who had also been the nurse of the Ilkhan Gaikhatu and honored in his court, as well as the grandmother of the Ilkhan Baidu. I thank Stefan Kamola for consultation on this point.

232. This is a river in northwestern Iran that flows into Lake Urmia from the south.

called *qāyājīs*[233] (that is, those who climb mountains and their peaks), shot arrows at them and killed a famous man. Battle and hatred occurred, sedition increased, evil grew, and ill will and grudges were increasing on both sides, Christian and Muslim. They made ambushes for each other, people prepared for battle, and the citadel's bridge was cut off. This was not by chance, but because that son of destruction, the cursed Nawruz, had gone to Khorasan intending to rebel against the kingship and seize it. He had stationed supporters in every place and partisans in all regions, but finally God revealed his tricks and uncovered his plots: while the Muslims were laying siege to the citadel, the cruel man's brother was seized, and so were his wives and his children. The victorious King Ghazan (may he be preserved in life) put them to death on the Sunday of the hymn *aynāw āsyā*, during the Savior's Fast of the Greek year 1608 [March 31, 1297].[234]

Trouble sprang up anew: the roads and paths were closed by those keeping guard over them, because that son of destruction had escaped, and the king's armies had gone out after him and were busy trying to capture him.

While they were chasing him, the Christians in the citadel of Arbil were being persecuted by those outside, who made siege mounds and battering rams and set up siege engines, preparing for a hard battle against the citadel. The metropolitan of Arbil was seized, whose name was Mar Abraham, an old man and ill,[235] along with many of the church's priests, clergy, and believers; some were killed, others sold for large sums. The citadel continued to be held under siege by the armies, some of them Mongols loyal to the emir who had done this, and some of them Kurds from various tribes. In short, they had come from all lands to plunder the

233. This rare term is formed from adding the Turkish suffix *-ji/chi* (referring to an occupation) to the Turkish word *qaya* (modern *kaya*), meaning "rock." The *qāyājīs* seem to have been non-Mongol soldiers in the Mongol armies, who were trained to fight in mountains. Their numbers included many Christians, such as Georgians and Armenians.

234. I.e., the sixth Sunday of Lent.

235. Or perhaps "an old man and an ascetic."

Christians; many murders took place because of this, and unspeakable captivities, and many from among the Muslims also died by the sword. This was the situation from the Monday of the Petition of the Ninevites until the Feast of the venerable Cross that same year [February 4 to September 13, 1297].[236]

This is how things were: the armies of the victorious king, with the great emir who was on his side, trapped that son of destruction inside a citadel in Khorasan.[237] The inhabitants of the citadel acted treacherously toward him, bound him, and handed him over, while tied up, to those armies. At that time they cut off his head and sent it to the victorious king. The messenger carrying it arrived on August 25 of that year; the victorious king was in a place called Sharb-khanah, in the vicinity of Ala Tagh. There was quiet after the waves of his evil and after the storms of his tricks and his plots. May he partake of the fate of Satan, his advisor and fellow servant.

As for the citadel of Arbil and the believers who were in it, rumors about them increased, and the uproar because of them grew strong in the great camp. It was said that they had killed many Muslims, had rebelled against the kingdom, and were killing every Ishmaelite[238] whom they met without mercy. Hatred grew and threatening increased, until the talk reached the ears of the victorious king and was repeated before

236. The Petition of the Ninevites (also called the Rogation of the Ninevites) refers to a three-day fast observed by the Church of the East on Monday through Wednesday, three weeks before the beginning of Lent, commemorating the preaching of Jonah to Nineveh in the Bible and a plague in Iraq in the 500s CE alleviated by prayer. The Feast of the Cross commemorates the finding of the True Cross by Helena, the mother of Constantine, and the later dedication of Constantine's Church of the Holy Sepulcher in Jerusalem in 335 CE. The Church of the East celebrates the Feast of the Cross on September 13, while other churches observe it on September 14.

237. Nawruz took shelter in Herat, where he was betrayed as described. The emir commanding Ghazan's army was Qutlughshah, and the messenger who brought his head to Ghazan was named Pulad Qaya, although Rashid al-Din gives a different date (August 14) for Nawruz's execution.

238. This is another term used for Muslims, due to the traditional ancestry of the Arabs being traced from Ishmael, the son of Abraham in the Bible.

his throne. As we previously mentioned, God gave the Christians mercy in the king's eyes. He realized that they were oppressed, and even though he had strayed from the path of his fathers and had inclined toward a dogma that makes one's soul cruel,[239] he did not change his good opinion of them.

This was the recompense of those who had made him hear the talk against the citadel: since the *catholicos* had moved with the camp to Ala Tagh, forced by the events that had happened to him, because he had no resting place for his head anywhere,[240] the victorious king sent to him two of the great men who were before him, one who was called *khwāja* Rashid al-Din and with him the emir Tarmadad.[241] They said, "The king commands; let the *catholicos* listen to his command." The *catholicos* replied, "Yes! Who does not receive the commands of the king (may he live forever)?" Then they said, "The king commands: what would happen if the king brought the Christians out of the citadel, gave them land, water, and homes, and protected them from all those who might harm them, had them come here and exempted them from all tax burdens? How would this plan be, and what is your opinion on the subject? Because hostility has increased between the two dogmas, that of the Muslims and that of the Syrians, if things are left like this, many losses would overtake the kingdom in this, and others would plot harm if these things are left alone. What, then, does the *catholicos* say of this plan and the method of accomplishing it?"

He answered them when he heard this and his eyes had filled with tears, and his mouth expressed his sorrow, as he spoke bitterly, "I have heard the command of my lord the king; no one can turn aside from it or change its contents. But when I remember and make known what happened to me, the sky and the earth are compelled to weep. If it pleases you, and you require an answer from me to say to the victorious king,

239. Phrases like this indicate the author's bias against Muslims.

240. Cf. Matthew 8:20; Luke 9:58.

241. Rashid al-Din Hamadani (d. 1318) is the famous vizier and historian; the title *khwājā* is a Persian term of respect. The emir Tarmadad has not been identified.

I will say that I had a residence in Baghdad, with a church and an endowment that had been bestowed upon me; they were taken. The church in Maragha with its residence was torn down to its foundations, and everything that was placed in it was broken into, as you are aware. I escaped the murder, and my condition is plain. The church and residence in Tabriz are now an open space with no building, and all that was in it has been looted. As for the residence that was in the city of Hamadan and the church, their sites are not at all apparent. The residence and church in the citadel in Arbil remain, with a hundred souls, and even these you wish to scatter and plunder. Why does my life continue? Let my lord the king command me either to return to the East, where I came from, or to go to the land of the Franks, to end my life there!"

When those who had been sent heard this, it grieved them and their eyes filled with tears. They rose at once and hastily went to the victorious king, to whom they expressed the character of these replies. At once the king (may he live forever) commanded that the Christians inside the citadel should not be expelled from it, and if they lacked food, to provide it at the *dīwān*'s expense until the armies would come down at the beginning of winter.[242] But one of the emirs, a hateful man, held back, and he wrote and acted differently.

One thing that was urgently needed was the liberation of the citadel's inhabitants, oppressed and shut in. After much effort and continuous running back and forth, a command came out and messengers were commanded to go to Arbil and free the citadel's inhabitants. The *catholicos*, for his part, was to send with them to the fortress one of the bishops, so that perhaps by his mediation the gates of the citadel would be opened and the inhabitants would give themselves to reconciliation. After the *catholicos* sent away the envoys and the bishops who were with them, they reached Arbil on September 14 of that year [1297 CE]. They restored the citadel's drawbridge, entered, and freed the citadel's inhabitants.

---

242. The *dīwān* is the government bureaucracy, so Ghazan orders the administration to provide supplies. The ability of one emir to thwart the order shows the limits of rulers' power.

After much effort, vexation of spirit, and sorrow of heart, they reconciled them with the Muslims. The expenses were not small from the *catholicos* and from the local Christians, a sum of 10,000 *dīnār*s, not including what was given to the emir who did this with them from the residence, a sum of 15,000 *dīnār*s more. The document of reconciliation was signed by the chief of the Muslims, and that of the Christian reconciliation between them and the Muslims was signed by their metropolitan: an emir took both documents with him, and they were shown to the victorious king. Then another command was issued, ordering that the citadel should belong to the Christians, who were authorized to demand back all that had been taken from them. The evil ceased and reconciliation increased by the help of God and the pouring out of his mercy upon his creatures.

Nevertheless, the Muslims did not cease doing evil, seeking to harm the Christians, as they have always plotted. And indeed one of them, called Nasir al-Din, head of the *dīwān*,[243] brought out a decree of the king, that Christians were to pay the *jizya* and when they walk in the streets they should wear wide belts.[244] This evil was worse than all other evils, and many were killed in the "City of Peace."[245] Without delay the *jizya* was collected from them, that is, the head tax, and their waists were bound with wide belts. It is true to say that this was not a *jizya* but a complete robbery.

When the Christians were walking in the streets or between houses, people were insulting, ridiculing, and mocking them, while saying, "See, you wretched ones, what you resemble with those wide belts!" They did not omit any annoyances that could be done to them, until God had mercy on them and through his kindness lifted all burdens from them and took away from them these trials that had overtaken them and surrounded them.

243. This person is not identified.

244. Paying a special head tax and wearing a visible belt (Arabic *zunnār*) were two common discriminatory requirements for Christians and Jews living under Muslim rule, though the special belt was not universally required.

245. This is a name for Baghdad.

Mar Yahballaha Prospers and Completes the Monastery in Maragha

That winter [1297–98 CE] the *catholicos* traveled with the victorious king to Mughan, their winter location. From there he came to Tabriz with them and spent the summer at the camp, in case he might discreetly provide for the needs of the church and of himself, and to turn away the violence and the powerful contentiousness of hateful people and to soothe their anger. During that time, the victorious king commanded and a seal, like the great seal that had been plundered, with the same inscription, was received. He was also given a *sukur*, that is, a parasol. Rays of affection were beginning to shine from the king toward the *catholicos*.

He spent the winter of the Greek year 1610 [1298–99 CE] in the citadel of Arbil, since he had not seen them since the year mentioned earlier, 1605 [1293–94 CE], and he rejoiced in seeing them and spent a pleasant winter with them. The father's joy with his children was great, and the children's joy with their father, as they were coming out from labors, or rather trials, and had been freed from great calamity and strong grief.

When the winter had passed, in the month of April [1299 CE], the *catholicos* left for the camp and was received by the king at Ujan, his summer location. He rejoiced at the sight of him and honored him. He commanded him to return to Maragha, regardless of circumstances, and with this command, the *catholicos* entered the city on the Sunday of the hymn *hāw d-b-ītūtēh* [May 31]. He spent that summer in Maragha with much enjoyment in his residence.

In October of the Greek year 1611 [1299 CE], he went down with King Ghazan again to the regions of Arbil and Mosul. It was the victorious king's intention to subjugate the lands of Palestine and Syria. The patriarch spent the winter in the citadel of Arbil. During the entire winter he was diligent to prepare funds for the monastery that he founded.

When the victorious king returned from Palestine (he subdued and broke their armies, looted them, scattered, killed, and took prisoners, and did what he had planned), the *catholicos* went up with him to Azerbaijan

A woven Mongol silk tapestry, depicting a ruler seated below a *sukur* (parasol), with a Mongol on one side and a Muslim advisor in a turban on the other. Behind the ruler stand two attendants, one holding a staff and the other holding the parasol above the ruler's head. The outer edge includes an Arabic inscription.

again. He began building the monastery, and he devoted his entire energies to it until he completed it.

In September of that year [1300 CE],[246] the victorious King Ghazan came to the lord *catholicos* in Maragha and stayed with him for three days. The Christians' joy grew, and great was the king's affection for them, because he knew well that they were innocent with no ill will, and that they were free from any evil. With a cheerful heart he left him, because the *catholicos* served him well.

The king again went down into the regions of Arbil and Mosul in the winter of the Greek year 1612 [1300–1301]. The *catholicos* also went down with him and accompanied him to a place in the vicinity of Sinjar,

246. Years in the "Era of the Greeks" start on October 1 and end on September 30, so the same year by that reckoning is a different year CE.

then returned to spend the winter in the citadel of Arbil, until the victorious king's return, when he again went up with him. During the trip, the Kurds set an ambush for the lord *catholicos*. As he went by on the road, they shot arrows at him, and one reached his finger, wounding him lightly. The victorious king was upset by this and swore with all their oaths, "I will get revenge on those Kurds!"

Upon arrival in Maragha the *catholicos* went to the monastery of Saint John the Baptist he had founded and took with him the monks he had gathered, since it was his aim to complete its construction. He was saying, "If God has mercy on me, I shall finish it and consecrate it; this would be a great kindness to me from him!" God (may his honor be worshipped) helped him.

His purpose was fulfilled according to his desire, and that construction was completed with everything proper, including all the precious ornaments impossible to describe, the beautiful buildings, and the amazing gates. With cut stones its structures were raised and its foundations were laid. Its gateways he made from speckled stones, and the stairs likewise. What word can describe its greatness? And the location of its site possesses great comfort and is full of splendor. The curtains on the door of the altar, on the saints' shrines, and on the storage room are amazing and wonderful, of many-colored fabric interwoven with fine gold. Its wall is so high that scaling it is impossible. In all the monks' cells there is running water, with pipes to carry away sewage. In it there is a new patriarchal residence; his throne is also there today, since the patriarch never leaves the monastery, most ordinations are completed in it, and determinations (that is, church canons) are confirmed in it.[247] The relics of saints, whose names we are about to mention, are kept in it, and healings flow to all seeking refuge. Truly, though the church is dedicated to John the Baptist, with great care and diligence that surpasses description, the relics of other saints have been gathered in it and arranged to

247. The present tense suggests that this was written while Mar Yahballaha was still alive (before 1317). It describes certain duties of the *catholicos*, particularly ordaining new priests and bishops and making decisions that become the canon law of the church.

provide help for believers, shelter for the distressed, rest for the afflicted, and relief for the harassed. The holy shrines are arranged side by side.

The length of its sanctuaries, according to those who measured it, including the altar, is sixty cubits, and the width of the central sanctuary is twelve cubits.[248] The altar, the Holy of Holies, and the treasury are exceptionally large; the dome above the altar is entirely covered on the outside with green *qāshānī* tiles,[249] and a cross is placed at its head.

These are the names of the saints whose relics are enshrined there: of the blessed mother, Saint Mary, a small piece of the *phakialion* of her head, which the late Rabban Sawma brought from the lands of the Franks; relics of Saint John the Baptist, of the holy apostles Peter and Paul (may their prayers be for everyone), Saint Thomas the apostle, Saint George, the apostles Saint Addai and Saint Mari who converted the East, Saint Stephen, the holy martyr Saint Cyriacus, with the Forty Martyrs, Saint Simeon Bar Sabbaʿe, Saint John of Dailam, Saint Sergius and Saint Bacchus, Saint Shallita, Saint Saba the martyr, Saint Hnanishoʿ, Saint Samuel, Saint James the Dismembered, Saint Sliba, Saint Ishoʿsabran, Saint Elisha the proven martyr, the household of Saint Maʿnyo, and Shmuni and her children.[250] May their prayer help the world and protect the inhabited land from all harm!

---

248. A cubit is about a foot and a half, so the length given is ninety feet, and the width eighteen.

249. The fanciest glazed tiles available were made in the city of Qashan (now called Kashan) in central Iran.

250. Mary, John the Baptist, Peter and Paul, Thomas, and Stephen are all named in the New Testament. Addai and Mari are the saints credited with bringing Christianity to Mesopotamia. George, Cyriacus, the Forty Martyrs, and Sergius and Bacchus are saints from late antiquity, shared with the Greeks. Simeon Bar Sabbaʿe (d. 345), Saba (d. 360s), and James the Dismembered (d. 420) were martyrs under the Sasanian Persian Empire. John of Dailam was an Eastern Syriac monk, mystic, and author in the early 700s CE. Shallita is identified as an early monk, from the 300s CE (but probably legendary). Hnanishoʿ was an earlier *catholicos* (d. 698), and Ishoʿsabran (d. 610) a martyred metropolitan of Arbil. Shmuni is the traditional Eastern Syriac name for the mother of the Maccabean martyrs (2 Maccabees 7). It is unclear who this "Samuel" is, since Syriac Orthodox Christians venerated Samuel of Qarṭmin (d.

The *catholicos* consecrated it and placed the altar stone on the day of the holy feast of the venerable Cross, September 13 of the Greek year 1612 [1301 CE]. All of the blessed believers of Azerbaijan gathered on the feast day of its consecration, and they came bearing vowed offerings and tithes, each in proportion to his ability and everyone according to his age and position. They rejoiced very greatly.

The lord *catholicos* gave a great banquet, where he gathered people of all confessions. He took the cup to everyone and made everyone glad. He blessed them like King Solomon, when he completed that great temple of God and blessed the people of the Lord.[251]

The quantity of the costs for this monastery until its completion were 420,000 *zūzē*. To the bishops and monks, the architects, the carpenters, the craftsmen, and all those who had worked on it, he gave robes, to each according to his rank and his service.

Indeed, prayers and offerings are constant in it, and for all easterners it is an object of admiration and a refuge supplying help. The *catholicos* endowed the holy monastery with revenues from a village east of Maragha, called Dahabi,[252] which he had purchased for 11,000 *dīnārs*. He made it a *waqf*, that is, an endowment of the holy monastery. Also other land grants, gardens, vineyards, orchards, fields, and so forth, he conferred upon that holy monastery so that the proceeds from them, that is, the fruits from them, will provide for supporting the livelihood and the food of the monks, candlesticks, wax candles, and the repairs and maintenance of that holy place. He called that holy monastery the "King of Monasteries."

---

410), but it would be surprising for the Church of the East to do so. "Sliba" usually refers to the True Cross, so it is unclear who is referenced here, and a martyr named "Elisha" is similarly unknown. The Syriac text here reads "the household of Saint Maʿnyo," but a manuscript in the Vatican reportedly includes a commemoration of "the holy daughter of Maʿnyo," a difference of one letter in Syriac. There was a church dedicated to Maʿnyo in Arbil, but it is unclear whether Maʿnyo was the name of a female saint or of her father.

251. 1 Kings 8:14.

252. This town is unidentified.

May he receive his wages from the Lord, and may he repay him as the salary of his labor happiness in the kingdom of heaven, and a dwelling with the saints, the friends of our Lord Jesus Christ. May he place on his right[253] all who labored and participated with him in this great labor. Amen!

King Ghazan's Affection for Mar Yahballaha, and His Death

After this monastery was completed and consecrated, the lord *catholicos* went to Tabriz to the victorious King Ghazan, who welcomed him gladly and looked at him with joy, honoring him more than usual and raising him above his rank. He questioned him regarding his construction and his labor, and when the *catholicos* replied that it was completed in its splendor, the victorious king was delighted. The lord *catholicos* blessed him in front of those present. The king departed for Mughan for the winter. As for the lord *catholicos*, the king commanded him to stay in his monastery and spend the winter there, saying, "A new building is pleasant and beneficial to its owner, because of his great effort."

At the turn of the year, when the king returned from Ujan, the *catholicos* went to see him and bless him. That meeting was the most joyous, and more than on any previous occasion they were delighted to see each other. The king assigned him a seat to his right and gave him many presents, among which were a *paiza* and fine royal robes. He showed his sincere affection, which came from a heart well purified. The lord *catholicos* also thanked him, then returned to Arbil in the Greek year 1614 [1302–3], and from there went to Baghdad. For a long time, about nine years, he had not visited the great patriarchal throne. The main reason for his trip was that the victorious king had also determined to go there.

He left Arbil on the Friday after the Christmas feast of that year [December 28, 1302], and entered Baghdad on the night of the feast

253. Cf. Matthew 25:31–46.

of Holy Epiphany [January 5, 1303].[254] He celebrated the feast in the Court of the Romans;[255] the whole congregation rejoiced in him, but his joy was even greater.

After twenty days he left Baghdad and went to the city of Hilla, which is located on the side of Babylon, the city built by the Chaldean king Nebuchadnezzar,[256] in order to see King Ghazan there. Soon after his arrival he appeared before the king, on the day in which the Mongols celebrate the White Feast [January 21, 1303].[257] The king received him more gladly than words can tell; he asked him about the state of his affairs, and why he had taken the trouble of coming to see him. The lord *catholicos* replied those things that were fitting.

The king had decided to enter Palestine again and conquer and subjugate again those regions. After a few days, the lord *catholicos* saw the king again, so that he could return to Baghdad; the king gave him five precious robes, garments of the king,[258] and settled all his affairs as he asked.

The king entered those lands, and the *catholicos* instead returned to Baghdad, where he settled in the Court of the Romans. He stayed there for the rest of that winter, hoping to go up to Azerbaijan at the end of the Fast [i.e., Lent] and settle in the monastery he had built.

On April 10 during that year [1303 CE] he left Baghdad, the city of the patriarchal throne, and on May 13 he arrived in the city of Maragha and in peace he reached the monastery he had founded. Subsequently, on June 10, the victorious king came to this monastery. The lord *catholicos* went out in procession to welcome him, and gave a great banquet as

254. Epiphany is January 6, but days start at sundown of the evening before, as is shown by him arriving in time to celebrate the feast in Baghdad, so he arrived late on January 5.

255. The Court of the Romans was a residence of the *catholicos* before the Mongol period.

256. Cf. Daniel 4:30, though Babylon existed before Nebuchadnezzar.

257. The Mongol new year (called "White Moon" in Mongolian), in late January or early February, on which Mongols wore white clothing as an auspicious color.

258. It was an honor to receive one of the king's own royal robes as a gift.

appropriate for him, and for the kings, the emirs, and the great men of the kingdom. The king treated the lord *catholicos* with honor and raised his rank above everyone else's; he made good and exalted promises to him, and he took off the mantle from his body and clothed him. It was a great joy for all the believers.

The king spent the night in the monastery, and during that night, while he was sleeping, he saw three angels standing over him in a dream: one was dressed in red clothes, the other two in bright green clothes. They encouraged him and announced to him the healing of his ankle pain.[259]

On the following day, he brought out a magnificent cross of fine gold, in which were set precious stones of great value, and in it there was a relic of the venerable wood of the cross of our Lifegiver,[260] the very relic the lord pope of the Romans had sent as a sign of honor to the king. The king bestowed it as a gift on the lord *catholicos*. He told all those present about his dream, and he acknowledged, "Due to the blessings of this holy house I regained health!" He remained all day at the monastery, praising and extolling the lord *catholicos*.

He left for the place where he usually spent the summer, that is, Ujan. On June 20 of that year [1303 CE], the king (may he live in victory) sent the lord *catholicos* a famous horse that he himself had been riding, and a fine mantle, with his own courier, inquiring about the health of the lord *catholicos* and promising him all good things. Subsequently, that same year, in the month of August, the victorious king sent the lord *catholicos* glass and *qāshānī* dishes (in Persian, *gīnah*),[261] decorated with gold, for he had brought craftsmen from the city of Damascus and from Qashan. He made known his great love by sending such dishes.

259. An ancient and medieval Christian custom was to sleep in a church, hoping to have a dream that would reveal the future, for example, the resolution of some difficulty or (as in this case) the outcome of a health problem.

260. "Lifegiver" is a Syriac title for Jesus.

261. The city of Qashan (modern Kashan) in Iran produced glazed ceramic tile, which was used both for architectural decoration and, here, for dishes. *Gīnah* in Persian means "mirror," from the reflectiveness of the surface.

A manuscript painting of the mausoleum of Ghazan outside of Tabriz, early fourteenth century.

While the king stayed in the city of Tabriz, in the month of November in the Greek year 1615 [1303 CE], the lord *catholicos* went down as usual to the citadel of Arbil to spend the winter there. All the fathers from that land and the Christian great men gathered to him, and after the great feast of our Lord's Resurrection [Easter, March 29, 1304], the great emir came to him, to whom the administration of Diyar Bakr was entrusted.[262] In his company, he went up undisturbed and in great honor to the monastery he had built in Maragha. He arrived on the night of the Pentecost Feast [evening of May 16, 1304].

Five days later [May 22] bitter, terrible, indeed tragic news reached him: the victorious King Ghazan had passed away! He had actually died on the Sunday of Pentecost [May 17, 1304], toward evening, in

262. Diyar Bakr is a region of northern Mesopotamia, centered around the city of Amid (modern Diyarbakır in Turkey). At this time, the governance of Diyar Bakr was conducted by the Artuqid ruler Najm al-Din Ghazi of Mardin.

the area of the town of Sahand.[263] All the inhabitants of the regions of his domain mourned him greatly. His coffin was carried to the city of Tabriz, on the Sunday of the hymn *kulmedem sāʿar* [May 24, 1304], and was placed in the great dome that the late king had built in that place.[264]

King Öljeitü and Mar Yahballaha

Since the great emirs who were at the helm of the administration of his kingdom steered straight, no rebellion arose and no disorder occurred anywhere at all. They immediately sent for the brother of the deceased king, born of the same father, who was called King Öljeitü. He was then in the region of Khorasan; they summoned him and proclaimed him king that same year [1304], on July 12.

Because he had been baptized when he was little, in the time of his father King Arghun, and he often went to see the lord *catholicos* with his mother Örüg Khatun, who was Christian, he had acquired great familiarity with him and felt measureless affection for him. Therefore the *catholicos* rejoiced greatly at his arrival, and he thought and said that this king would honor the congregation more than his father and his brother, since he had seen and learned of their honor for him and their affection toward him. He did not realize that voluntary transformations are more powerful and overcome customary and natural habits, especially when they become rooted and spread. The king had become a Hagarene in those regions, and he had received a different education, as a consequence of which he had forgotten all the earlier things, and by the many conversations he had heard, some hatred toward Christians was found in him.

---

263. This is probably not the city named Sahand near Tabriz, because it took a week to transport Ghazan's body to the capital. There is a pair of villages named Sahand west of Zanjan, but Rashid al-Din reports Ghazan's place of death as Peshkala near Qazvin (unlocated, but presumably farther east of Zanjan).

264. Ghazan had commissioned a high-domed mausoleum outside of Tabriz at a place named Shamm.

When the lord *catholicos* went to him and met him twice, the king honored him, but not from the heart. Due to the power of the Shame he did not much desire to meet him,[265] for he gave a strong hand and a mighty arm to the Hagarenes in every way, with gifts, decrees, honors, and the building of mosques, and from this fact they trampled underfoot the church things. At once their evil came and grew strong, until they insinuated in King Öljeitü's ears that they could take the monastery built by the *catholicos* and turn the church of the city of Tabriz into a mosque, and the *waqf* (that is, land grants) of the church would belong to the mosque.

This very nearly happened, but for the divine help and divine kindness that stirred up the exalted emir Irinjin (may he be preserved in life), the king's maternal uncle,[266] who hindered their boldness and restrained their daring. Otherwise they would have seized even the monastery that he had built.

The winter of the Greek year 1616 [1304–5 CE] was spent by the *catholicos* in the town of Ushnuviya.[267] Even there he barely escaped from the hands of the rebels and came to the monastery he had built. From there he went to the camp in Ujan, and he entered Tabriz with the king. He strove to improve the church's situation, received a decree,[268] and returned to the monastery. He then departed from there to spend the winter in the citadel of Arbil. With his arrival, at the beginning of the Greek year 1617 [October 1305 CE], he founded a great residence in the citadel itself, built it of lime and plaster, and completed it and decorated it with all beauty.

At the beginning of the month of May of that year [1306 CE] he went to the monastery he had built to spend the summer there. When he

265. This obscure phrase is here interpreted to mean that the power of Öljeitü's conversion to Islam (which the author labels "the Shame") led the Ilkhan not to seek the presence of the *catholicos*.

266. Irinjin (d. 1319) was the brother of Öljeitü's mother, Örüg Khatun.

267. A town near Urmia in northwestern Iran, also known as Ushnuq or Ashnukh.

268. This is again a Mongol *yarligh* granting certain privileges to the *catholicos* and his community.

heard that the king had begun to take the *jizya* from Christians, he went to Ujan again. He met the king but did not achieve anything.

The king then began to build a city near the borders of Qazvin, which he completed and named Sultaniyya.[269] He gathered there craftsmen from all the lands of his empire, and he decorated it with splendid buildings and with indescribable style.

Because the lord *catholicos* had no source of income, and his expenses were many, he went again to the citadel of Arbil, to the residence he had built. He spent the winter there in the Greek year 1618 [1306–7 CE], then the summer and again the winter of the year 1619 [1307–8 CE]. At the start of May [1308] he went up to Azerbaijan. He went to the king in the city of Ujan and was treated with the honor according to his rank and custom.

The king rode out to hunt and came to the holy monastery built by the lord *catholicos*. The monks went out to meet him and brought him in with pomp. He entered the cell of the superior of the monastery, who found mercy in his eyes. The king asked him about the mysteries of the Christians,[270] and he replied well and even beautifully. The king rejoiced greatly, entered the cell of the *catholicos*, and sat on his throne. He summoned the monks and rejoiced with them, and he gave them five fine robes. There the superior spoke about the *jizya* to him, and he promised not to take it anymore. He did not burden the monastery with anything.

After he departed the next day, the *catholicos* heard and came to the monastery, and was very sad that he was not present in the monastery. He followed after the king and met him on the bank of the river called Jaghatu in Mongolian, and Vakyarud in Persian,[271] and the bishops and the superior of the monastery were with him. The king honored the lord *catholicos* beyond his power, and he permitted a great decree of stipulations to be written for him, regarding him and the Christians, in which he ordered that no one should require the *jizya* from bishops, from monks,

269. Modern Soltaniyeh, near Zanjan.

270. The conversation was probably mostly on the topic of sacraments.

271. This is a river in northwestern Iran that flows into Lake Urmia from the south.

priests, or deacons in all the territory of his kingdom. When the *catholicos* returned to the monastery, the king again summoned him to Tabriz, and he gave him a mule for riding and a precious mantle. From the time when he entered the monastery, the knot of the king's heart was untied and God put mercy in his heart. He gave the *catholicos* permission to spend the winter in the monastery, and the king went to his winter location at Mughan.

The *catholicos* thus spent the winter in the monastery, and also the summer of the Greek year 1620 [1308–9]. The king had mercy with favorable decrees, and he even granted the *jizya* of all of Arbil to the *catholicos* and commanded that the *jizya* not be taken from Christians again.

As soon as the *catholicos* left for the citadel of Arbil, in the month of November of the Greek year 1621 [1309], he became deathly sick along the way, but our Lord gave him health. He entered the citadel of Arbil with pomp, when the whole city had come out to meet him, and they brought him in with great honor.

The Massacre of Arbil's Christians[272]

Since the completion of divine decrees is inevitable, and as for the occasions of God's amazing providence, apart from them the decrees would be unfulfilled, at that time he caused some people among the mountaineers who were from the *qāyājīs* (that is, those who climb the height of mountains)[273] to quarrel with one another. Some of them went to the king with accusations against their emir, Zayn al-Din Balu, in

272. For historical background to this episode, see pp. 16–17 of the Introduction.

273. The *qāyājīs* seem to have been non-Mongol soldiers in the Mongol armies who were trained to fight in mountains. Their numbers included many Christians, such as Georgians and Armenians. See pp. 106–7 for the role of the *qāyājīs* in Arbil in 1297.

The center of the city of Arbil in northern Iraq is a large, heavily fortified citadel, built in an oval shape over a thousand feet long and wide, on top of a mound that is eighty to one hundred feet higher than the rest of the city. This photograph shows the rocky slope and more recent buildings on top.

whose hands the salaries for three thousand men were administered.[274] The king was angry at him and held him in prison for a year. Because of him, the victorious king sent to the citadel of Arbil a Muslim man, ill-starred and bitter of disposition, who was called Nasir.[275] He was the cause of the completion of the Muslims' inclination that began in the Greek year 1608 [1297 CE]. All the children of Hagar,[276] great and small, noble and humble, emirs and troops, scribes and lawyers, governors and counselors, conspired to seize the citadel of Arbil from the Christians and to destroy its inhabitants.

---

274. The accusation seems to be that this commander was mismanaging funds so that the soldiers were not getting paid. This emir does not seem to be otherwise known.

275. Our only other source for these events, the *History of Öljeitü* by Abu l-Qasim ʻAbdallah al-Qashani, mentions him as Nasir Dilqandi.

276. I.e., the Muslims. Notice that the author's assertion of a universal plot is a conspiracy theory that reflects his anti-Muslim bias.

On the other hand, it is right to tell the truth, that the inhabitants of the citadel, and the others who were with them, were hard-hearted and had directly left the path of Christianity, and they entirely neglected the divine laws, mocked the recluses and priests, and wronged one another. They were so used to transgressing the precepts of the Lord that there was no longer any place among them for admonishment, nor for teaching, for hatred had grown inside them and enmity had taken hold of their hearts. They were accusing one another, oppressing, beating, persecuting, holding grudges, and wronging one another. They formed factions and attacked the homes of their chiefs. In short, they made space for doing all sorts of evil. No one was bringing to mind or fearing the hard anger and punishment [of God].

But events such as these are of divine origin, which providence accomplishes when it takes the opportunities, just as when God decreed death for Adam because of his transgression of the command,[277] or when he hardened the heart of Pharaoh to punish him,[278] and other things like these may be said as examples, but the purpose of providence, as in Pharaoh's case, is: "For this very reason have I raised you up, to make known my power in you, and that my name may be proclaimed in all the earth,"[279] and according to this other verse: "The Lord hardened the heart of Pharaoh so that he would not know him,"[280] to make known his miracles and mighty acts on the earth.

These same things happened to the hearts of the mountaineers, known as *qāyājīs*; the inhabitants of the Arbil citadel became stubborn, and they were abandoned by divine help, so that the fearsome aspects of providence might become known and the secret things of his glorious nature might be learned. But also, although God (may his honor be worshipped) knows the direction of a human's inclinations before he

277. Cf. Genesis 2:17; 3:17–19.

278. Cf. Exodus 9:12; 10:1, 20, 27; 11:10; 14:8.

279. Romans 9:17; cf. Exodus 9:16.

280. Ecclesiasticus/Ben Sira 16:15.

brings him into existence, he admonishes him when he elicits them, as his foreknowledge knows and administers.

This Nasir whom we mentioned above, from the time when he entered the citadel, stayed in a tower beside the gate and did not go out again. Instead, he was bringing up individual weapons of war and men secretly, and he was sending word to the camp that these were *yāghīs* (that is, enemies of the king), because their emir was held in prison. As for the citadel's inhabitants, the more he acted in this manner, the more openly they demonstrated their evil. But they were not harmful to him at all, because on his side he had the whole people, more or less, and the gold of all Muslims, while on their side there was not even opportunity for one of them to help another with one penny.[281] Nasir had advice like Ahithophel's[282] from all the scribes and all the chiefs, but they had no one, because they were drunk with wine and were out of their minds both from the abundance of divine abandonment and from their evil actions that they had done, and they were not afraid of the Lord's just and righteous judgments.

What happened then? The king's messengers were coming and going: "Arise and come down from the citadel, Christians." As for them, it was not at all decided for them to obey but to rebel, and the more they were doing this, the more the Muslim people were rejoicing and being glad, since there were signs that their goal was being fulfilled and realized.

When the disaster grew strong, a royal command was issued to an emir named Sutai, who was in those regions of Diyar Bakr.[283] A man named Hajji Dilqandi brought it, the brother of the Nasir mentioned, the one who was settled inside the citadel.[284] The decree ordered the

---

281. The term used here (*shmōnā*) indicates a very small coin of little value.

282. Cf. 2 Samuel 16:23.

283. Sutai Akhtachi was a powerful emir who had married a granddaughter of Hülegü. Diyar Bakr refers to the region of Upper Mesopotamia.

284. "Hajji" is an honorific title for a Muslim who has completed the pilgrimage (*ḥajj*) to Mecca, although in the case of Dilqandi (d. 1318), his "pilgrimage" consisted of

qāyājīs to leave the citadel; otherwise, the citadel was to be overpowered and subjugated by force, and the king's armies were to be gathered against it to prepare for the attack.

As for the *catholicos*, due to his love for the kingdom, he did not imagine that while he was dwelling in the citadel, this was being done in the citadel, nor did the Christians imagine that they would be treated like this while the *catholicos* was with them, and all of them neglected what was obligatory, including going to the camp and making known what had happened to them. They remained submerged in the sleep of negligence, until things they never thought would happen overtook them.

On the day of Wednesday, March 9 of that year [1310],[285] during the Savior's Fast [i.e., Lent], the son of this emir who was mentioned,[286] accompanied by three commanders of thousands, went up to the *catholicos* to bring him down. He was told that if he did not leave with them, he would be imprisoned. The following day he left under compulsion, and from then on, fear and weeping came upon the citadel, and bad omens also appeared. They led him to the monastery of Saint Michael of Tarʿel, and the emir Sutai visited him, and the armies that were with him, with the commanders of thousands and the rest. The emir showed much affection for him, since many times he had come to the patriarchal residence and had been a true friend, and he had been highly honored by the lord *catholicos* in the time of the deceased King Ghazan. He said to the *catholicos*, "The command is for the mountaineers to come down from the citadel, while the others shall remain within. Since they certainly will not come out, except by your command, you will send them one of your people to lead them out."

---

leading the Ilkhan's army to Mecca in 1316. Thus using his title "Hajji" for events in 1310 is anachronistic.

285. Oddly, unlike other references to days of the week, in this case the day of the week does not match the date. In 1310, March 9 was a Monday. Either March 9 is the correct date, and there were more days than the narrative includes, or Wednesday was the correct day, but the date was March 11.

286. It is uncertain which son of Sutai is mentioned here.

The *catholicos*, on the following morning (it was a Friday), had oxen, sheep, and wine sent to the residence of the emir mentioned. He put a cup in his hands, according to Mongol custom, and mounted him on a good horse, in order to quiet his mind. The Muslims that were present, Hajji Dilqandi, the Shaykh Mahmud, Arbil's governor, and his brother, called Ahmad, were clamoring against the Christians, and even against the *catholicos*: "No one will bring them down from the citadel except you!"[287] But the emir, thinking of the bribe given to him by the *catholicos*, ignored them.

They agreed to send someone to [the mountaineers] to advise them to come down. The *catholicos* sent one of the bishops who were with him, called Mar ʿAbdishoʿ, the bishop of Hanitha, and the emir sent one of the commanders of thousands, called Sati Beg,[288] to speak with them so that they would come down. But when they went and spoke with all gentleness, making good promises, [the mountaineers] did not accept or obey. They then returned to those who had sent them, on Saturday, March 14. As soon as the emir Sutai heard, he came to the *catholicos* and spoke with him, saying, "These are *yāghīs* (that is, enemies)! Send word again, *catholicos*, to them a second time." The lord *catholicos* wrote an exhortation to the effect that they should come down, and he sent it by the bishops Mar Ishoʿsabran the metropolitan and Mar ʿAbdishoʿ, who was mentioned, and the monks Rabban David, a recluse, and Rabban Denha, superior of the monastery of Saint Michael of Tarʿel. They left on the night leading into the Sunday of the hymn *enhū d-teʿōl* [March 15], and when it dawned, they entered the citadel. The people of the citadel spoke with them, and they consented to come down.

When Nasir heard of this, immediately he gave the signal that he had arranged between him and the people of the city, that when he

287. I.e., while the emir Sutai was asking the *catholicos* to achieve a negotiated resolution, these people are appealing to Sutai to end the standoff unilaterally by force of arms.

288. This is not the Sati Beg who was ruling queen of the Ilkhanate during the factionalism of the late 1330s.

raised it upon the roof of the tower in which he was dwelling, they were to go up to him and prepare for battle.

When these poor people, who had taken counsel in the church to go down, saw the swords glitter and sharp arrows rain down, with difficulty they hurried and went to the gate of the citadel. They too made battle from ten in the morning[289] until the evening and all night. Three Muslim men were killed and twelve of the Christians, and if they had not put fire at the foot of that tower for the entire night, they would have all been killed without hindrance. Upon hearing the news, the emir Sutai and the troops that were with him left in all haste to surround the citadel, and by force they took with them the *catholicos*, weeping. On the same day, they arrived at the base of the citadel, while saying to him, "Do not allow them to prepare for battle."

Some of them came down from the citadel on the night between Sunday and Monday, and God saved them. The *catholicos* was with them, imprisoned, and the bishops who were with him. On the Monday [March 16], at the break of day, again the emir Sutai and his men forced the lord *catholicos* to send them a message for them to allow Nasir to come down with all that he had. He sent the reverend Ishoʿsabran and Rabban David the recluse. As soon as the Muslims saw them, they killed Rabban David the recluse without mercy; as for Ishoʿsabran, they struck him with swords and clubs, but God saved him from their hands and he escaped and came back.

The calamity got worse, since punishment had come. From then on, the Muslims and Mongol armies began to make siege mounds and siege engines of various kinds to prepare for battle.

As for the Christians in the lower city,[290] ever since Nasir had raised that evil sign, they were being killed in the city's streets and squares. Many fled and entered into the houses of Muslims, but even those were

289. "The fourth hour of the day" counting from dawn, near the spring equinox, would be approximately 10:00 a.m.

290. I.e., in Arbil, outside the citadel.

brought out by means of heralds,[291] and on that Monday they died without mercy in a bitter massacre. Some who were in the prison of their *qāḍī* were led out with bitter scourging until they received death. The young women were stripped bare and made to go around the streets of the city. They were ripping open wombs and killing the babies. They were throwing their corpses in front of the citadel's gate, and coming to tell the emir Sutai, "Emir, send someone to see how they kill the Muslims and throw them by the gate of the citadel!" He, in his simplicity, believed them and gave a command, and the four churches in the lower city were destroyed (two of ours,[292] one dedicated to the illustrious martyr Isho'sabran,[293] and one dedicated to Ma'nyo; the Jacobite church,[294] dedicated to Saint Mary, and the Armenian church) down to the ground, and all the houses and courtyards of the Christians and the residence of the metropolitan's throne.[295]

The emir sent messengers to the whole district and gathered men to prepare for battle. They made the Kurds come down from the mountains. The Christians, because they could not go to the city, gave no small amount of silver from all the villages for the weapons and food of the armies. Battle raged against the citadel on all four sides, night and day. Many of the defenders and attackers were killed, including Kurds and Muslims, but not Mongols, since they were not going near the citadel, but only shooting arrows from afar.

Routes were cut off for the Christians, there and everywhere else. Wherever people would see them, they would kill them without mercy, saying, "You are from the citadel!" or "These are fugitives!" Terror of death seized everyone. As for the *catholicos*, none of those holding him

---

291. It is unclear if these heralds were announcing safety for the Christians or threats to those who shelter them.

292. I.e., belonging to the Church of the East.

293. This is not the metropolitan mentioned recently but was instead a martyred metropolitan of Arbil (d. 610). For the ambiguity around the name Ma'nyo, see n. 250.

294. "Jacobite" is a derogatory term for the Western Syriac denomination whose patriarch claimed the patriarchate of Antioch.

295. I.e., residence of the metropolitan of Arbil.

continued to help him in practice, and few even in words. They guarded him closely at night and from a distance during the day, and he had no idea what would happen to him. His thoughts were distracted with fear for himself and for the citadel; he hardly had the space to write to the metropolitan of Arbil, who had fled to the village of Beth Sayyade. The metropolitan, angry at the people of the citadel because they had not listened to him, had departed for Beth Sayyade with all his belongings and was hidden there. The *catholicos* said to him, "What does your escape benefit you, if you do not go to the camp?"[296] Two days later, the emir Sutai sent guards with the *catholicos*, and they led him to Beth Sayyade.

The metropolitan left on the very night the letter reached him, and within four days he reached Baghdad with the boy who was with him. He went to the camp and made known what had happened to the *catholicos* and the Christians. By then the emirs in the camp had already heard all that had taken place, because the emir Sutai had sent messengers to let the court know what had been done by him. The *catholicos* had also sent a letter through a messenger to one of the servants of the patriarchal residence, to report what had happened to him, and the servant had gone and made known to the emirs and advisors and informed them of the message, and notified them about the massacre that happened. Those from among the emirs who were unaware of this situation were very sympathetic, but those who had been involved in the matter were silent. Soon afterward, the metropolitan arrived hurrying and on foot, and he repeated the same message to all the emirs. A royal command was written to the emir Sutai through a messenger: "This is what you reported to us, but the *catholicos* reports otherwise. Which of you should we believe and be convinced by?" The calamity was held back a little.

Sutai, when he heard this message, was very annoyed and became angry. He sent for the *catholicos* and had him brought. (He asked him,) "Did you write this?" All the Muslim people were clamoring against the

296. Since the *catholicos* is kept under guard, he cannot go to the Ilkhan Öljeitü to intercede for the Christians, so he hints that this metropolitan should go, since he has the ability. This metropolitan is the most likely author of this text.

catholicos, and each of them was shouting whatever came to their minds. The *catholicos* said, "I wrote nothing, but Metropolitan So-and-so of this place went and spoke on behalf of his household and his flock."[297]

They said, "Now make these rebels come down, in compliance with the royal decree, or else write a letter that they are *yāghīs*." The *catholicos* sent to them the metropolitan of Mosul and a few boys from the patriarchal residence, and they urged the people of the citadel, but they were afraid to come down. There were some real rebels among them, who, from fear of being killed, were making others rebel so that they would not go down. Then the emir Sutai and his supporters had the advantage over the *catholicos*, and they pressed him: "Give us a letter stating that they are *yāghī*, so we can send a messenger to inform the king." They robbed and took all that he had with him, and they killed some of those who had come down to him and sold others. By force, they obtained a document signed by him and by the bishops who were with him, as they desired.

On that same day, emir Sutai sent Hajji Dilqandi (he was close)[298] to the king. As soon as he arrived, he made known the message. One of the emirs, called Esen Qutlugh,[299] rebuked him firmly and restrained his impudence, because he knew the truth and perceived that that document had been extorted by force. He wanted to hit him, but Hajji Dilqandi escaped. The emir Esen Qutlugh entered with all the counselors and informed the king. The latter ordered the inhabitants of the citadel and the Muslims to be reconciled. No one was to take revenge from one side or the other, and also no one was to make war.

---

297. Mar Yahballaha denies responsibility and ascribes it to the pastoral concern of the metropolitan. This is the only place in the text where anyone is called "so-and-so," although the name must have been known to both Mar Yahballaha and the author. This is circumstantial evidence that this metropolitan is the author, since excluding one's own name from what one writes was considered a praiseworthy mark of humility.

298. It is unclear whether this means that Hajji Dilqandi was a relative of Sutai (or of the king), was a close friend of his, or was just convenient to send.

299. Esen Qutlugh (d. 1318) was one of the dozen or so most powerful emirs during the reign of Öljeitü.

This decree was produced only after many efforts, troubles, and anxieties of the metropolitan and his companions. It was delivered to some of the royal princes to take it to Arbil. Hajji Dilqandi went back in shame, with his face blushing. Two of the disciples of the patriarchal residence also came with the decree, and they reached Arbil on the Friday of the Confessors [April 24]. They immediately rejoined the citadel's drawbridge, which had been burned, and they made peace. Many came down from the citadel into the country.

But, as was mentioned earlier, the Muslims had given to Nasir and his brother as much gold as they wished to expend in bribes. They satisfied these messengers who had brought the decree with feasting, then suggested they go up to the citadel. When they went up, no one gave them a carpet to sit on, nor were they given to eat even a piece of bread, nor did they give them even one penny.

Then the messengers regretted having made peace, and they returned again to an evil and bitter disposition. They desired to do harm to the boys of the patriarchal residence who had accompanied them. One of them fled from them through the citadel's gate secretly to the village of Beth Sayyade. They chased after him but did not find him, so they caught his companion and guarded him. The messengers pursued and came to the village of Beth Sayyade, and they summoned the *catholicos* and repeated the message, "These people will not come out, unless at your order. Come, obey the decree!"

When the *catholicos* reached Arbil, all the Muslim people gathered around Sutai and began speaking harshly with the *catholicos*. Due to the great trust that he had in the kingdom, he was returning harsh answers to them.[300] The *catholicos*, along with the emir Sutai, sent a second message to the citadel's inhabitants, that they should come down and take an oath on the Gospel that they would not harm Nasir. He would also take an oath to them, and they would be reconciled. After many came down and swore that they would not harm him and that they would submit to him

300. I.e., he did not feel the need to answer with flattery or even politeness, because he assumed that the king's court would support him against his accusers.

as he desires, and after it was confirmed that he was going up with three hundred men, the gate was locked again, because their hearts were full of deceit.[301]

When he saw this, Sutai seized those who had descended and they killed them. The companion of the one who had escaped, of the boys of the patriarchal residence, was interrogated regarding his companion with many blows, and the *catholicos* barely managed to rescue him. They captured the mares and mules belonging to the patriarchal residence, and all the possessions of the boys and the bishops who had come with the *catholicos*, including their clothes. They then said to him with deceit, "We will bring to you the powerful men of the city in the square below the citadel, so that no one quarrels again and is incited to wage war, until we inform the victorious king." In simplicity, he accepted and went up to the citadel, unaware of the trap the Muslims had made for him, in order to kill him.[302]

On that day, a messenger came to the emir Sutai from his home:[303] "The armies of Palestine have entered the regions, and if you fail to come, even your household might be led into captivity." Immediately all the armies with him departed, even though he was suffering from a serious illness. No one remained at the foot of the citadel except the Kurds and the people of the city.

The following day, battle and killing began between the two sides. The routes were cut off, and no one was going or coming, nor was anyone carrying away news or bringing it. The famine grew strong in the citadel, and anyone who came out either to flee or to bring provisions to his household was killed without pity. The *catholicos* and three bishops who

301. By locking the gate against Nasir, the commander appointed by the Ilkhan, the people in the citadel were appearing to back out of the agreement.

302. The trap is that if the *catholicos* is tricked into the citadel and shut in with the rebels, he can be accused of inciting rebellion against the king without an opportunity to respond to the allegations, as in fact is described below.

303. That is, from the region of Diyar Bakr in Upper Mesopotamia. The "armies of Palestine" would refer to the forces of the Mamluk Empire, which ruled Syria and Palestine from Cairo in Egypt.

were with him, and the boys who were left with him, were locked into the citadel without covering and without bedding, without food and without provisions. Punishment was becoming harsher, anxiety increased, and terror grew strong; there was no helper or refuge left, nor anyone able to help with a word.

Those messengers returned to the camp with Hajji Dilqandi and informed the king that the people were *yāghīs* and the *catholicos* had made them rebel, and that he gave a bribe and went up to the citadel, where he had opened the treasuries for them and distributed gold, brought out the stored grain, as well as weapons of war, ropes, and war machines, and had strengthened them to prepare for battle.

Evil was decided in the heart of the king and his great men. Decrees were issued again, thirteen in number, addressed by name to each emir of the Kurds and the four emirs of the king of the Mongols, with one for the whole region of Arbil, that if anyone should bring food into the citadel or give them food, that village would be plundered and killed, and if they owned land in the area, it would be confiscated and become the king's property. The emirs, with strong equipment, were to make war for the sake of the triumph of the Ishmaelite confession.[304] A separate decree was addressed to the *catholicos*, who was commanded by it: "We and our fathers have honored you so that you would pray for us and bless us, but now that you are acting otherwise, you are responsible for what is coming upon you, not ourselves." They entrusted the decrees to one of those in the royal court, called Toghan, and to Hajji Dilqandi, both of whom were truly enemies of all Christianity, so that they would go to Arbil and fulfill their will.

The metropolitan of Arbil, after the earlier messengers were sent to make peace accompanied by the two boys from the patriarchal residence, remained at the camp for three days. Then he thought, "If the people of the citadel and the Muslims reconcile, there is no benefit from staying at the camp, and if they quarrel again, I will not be able to say anything without the advice of the *catholicos*." Immediately he arose and

304. I.e., Islam.

came rapidly to the village of Beth Sayyade. On his arrival, he found that the *catholicos* had been escorted out on the same day, along with the bishops who were with him, as was made known above, and he had been locked inside the citadel. All the Christians were standing in grief, afflicted and sad, a sadness from the heart, not the one some people display on their eyebrows and eyelids, but the one that melts the flesh and dissolves the bones, because they did not know what would happen to them at the hands of the Muslims, and whether they would be freed from that punishment or not. Like those who are shipwrecked at sea among the waves and the storms, they too feared drowning in the destruction of the punishment.

The metropolitan mentioned was unable to endure it; he thought again of returning to the camp, but he hesitated, because the roads were blocked off and he had no companions at all, and there was no opportunity to consult with the *catholicos*, and if he would stay in his residence while the *catholicos* and the bishops were afflicted and mistreated and the Christians tormented, he would have become guilty before the canon of truth and the law of Christ, that both a shepherd and a friend must lay down his life and give oneself to death,[305] must despise life and endure all torments for the love of Christ. So he was strengthened and took with him the boys of the residence who had fled and were hiding.[306] They left the village of Beth Sayyade on the evening of May 6 of that year [1310].[307] They walked all night and day across mountains and plains, hills and valleys, fearful and trembling from the ambushes of the enemies, without shelter and without enough food.

With God's help, they arrived ten days later in the city of Hamadan, since they had heard the king was there. But when they entered the city, on that very day the victorious king had left and went to their capital

305. Cf. John 10:11; 15:13.

306. It is not clear whether his companions were those associated with the patriarch's residence, or those associated with his own residence, that of the metropolitan of Arbil.

307. Since days start in the evening, this would be late on May 5 in Western reckoning.

Öljeitü built his massive mausoleum in his new capital city, Sultaniyya.

city. The metropolitan and the boys left on the following day and went to Sultaniyya, and they heard that those decrees had been given to the two people mentioned above, Toghan and Hajji Dilqandi, and they were ready to leave and go to Arbil. Hearing this, their hands faltered, their knees shook, and their eyes shed tears for the breaking of the church and what had befallen her children. They sought advice on what to do from certain people, friends of the *catholicos* and of the people of the church, and received the reply, "Do not spare your belongings, nor those of the residence, otherwise the *catholicos* will perish and so will you; the churches will be looted and even the *waqf* of the Christians will be gone because of the *catholicos*."

The metropolitan immediately took with him some money and went to one of the emirs, someone who was very close to the king. The emir received him with honor and listened to what he had to say about the *catholicos* as well as the Christians. The emir accepted a document from the metropolitan, containing everything that he said, and showed it to the emirs and the king (may God make him victorious), just as will be made known later. The emir handed the metropolitan over to three well-known men who were with him, to lead him to each one of the emirs and the viziers that stand before the king, so he could say orally what he had written. Those men brought him to an emir called Esen Qutlugh, then to *khwāja* Saʿd al-Din, the chief scribe, and the vizier *khwāja* Rashid al-Din.[308]

The metropolitan confidently said the message, which was this: "The lord *catholicos* greets you and says, 'You know, emirs, that it is thirty-five years since I arrived from the East, that I was seated on this eastern [patriarchal] throne by the will of God, and that I have served and blessed seven kings, with all patience and the fear of God, especially the father of the present victorious king, the late Arghun, and his mother Örüg Khatun, the believer. I have not betrayed anyone. Any of the possessions of the kingdom I have not desired. If any alms were given to me by them, I also was spending it on them. I was young then, and now I am old, and I have no children or wife, or relatives near or distant, that any love of this world might lead me to rebel against the king, or contemplate stealing anything of his. How then can my enemies' accusations against me be believed? Have I been harmed by this king (may God make him victorious)? Far from it! But even if it were the case that he had done any harm to me—far from it!—I am commanded to repay good instead of evil in the holy gospel, the book that I profess, when it says, 'Pray for your enemies and bless those who curse you, and do good to those who hate you.'[309] I am not able to renounce anything that I have been commanded by God through his Christ, since the transgression of a command makes someone alienated, whoever he may be, from the one who made the command.[310] I beg you, that if the king is certain in his heart that I have done evil, bring me to the royal court and make known to me exactly what I have done, and then I will deserve death and he will

308. Esen Qutlugh and Rashid al-Din were introduced earlier. Saʿd al-Din Sawaji (d. 1312) shared top-level bureaucratic roles with Rashid al-Din during the reigns of Ghazan and Öljeitü.

309. Cf. Matthew 5:44.

310. Here the reasoning applies simultaneously to transgressing God's command in the gospel book and to disobeying Öljeitü's command as king, implying that Mar Yahballaha is obedient to both.

be innocent of my blood, but do not let him leave me in the hands of my enemies!' This is the message of the *catholicos*.[311]

"All the Christians inside the citadel are saying, 'We are not rebels against the victorious king, but we are very afraid of our enemies. The Kurds and the Muslims are killing us without pity. No one has mercy on us and we have no one to make known to the king the affliction we are in. We are his servants and subjects. We always pay the tribute and taxes imposed on us. So if the king commands us to make the *qāyājīs* come down, with whom his heart is occupied, will we be able to do this?[312] If he commands us to come down from the citadel, let him send someone to save us from the hands of these tyrants, and wherever he wishes, let him command us to go, since we have not stayed here by the pleasantness of the place, but rather by our great fear of the Palestinians and Kurds.[313] See, our sons and our daughters have been led into captivity, and most of the men have been killed.'

"Emirs, you are all aware of these things, and I, your servant the metropolitan, guarantee to you what I said, as well as the document that I wrote and delivered."

The emirs received the message and showed it to the victorious and compassionate king. He commanded the emir of emirs, Chupan,[314] to investigate the situation, have the metropolitan brought to him, and

---

311. The metropolitan of Arbil is putting these words in the mouth of Mar Yahballaha, because he has not had the opportunity to consult with him. He continues his message by speaking in the voice of the besieged Christians in the citadel of Arbil, and then speaking in his own voice.

312. The implicit answer is no, but the text does not in fact read "we are not able to do this," so I have interpreted it as a question.

313. If the previous mention of the "Palestinian armies" referenced the Mamluks, it is unclear what "Palestinians" are intended here. It may refer to Syrian Arab residents in Arbil.

314. The title "emir of emirs" (Arabic *amīr al-umarāʾ*) is given to a top general. In this case, Chupan (also spelled Choban) did not receive this title until years after the events described, but he was already a leading general, and after Öljeitü's death in 1316, he became the regent for the young new Ilkhan, Abu Saʿid.

speak with him. When they brought him, he spoke all the things that he had repeated, and he added, "Because of you, all these things were done among us," for Chupan had a link to the emir of the *qāyājīs*, the one called Balu. Chupan received the message readily, and he stopped Hajji Dilqandi from traveling to Arbil. He made good promises and set apart some messengers to go, different from the original ones.

Meanwhile, so that we do not prolong the story, Hajji Dilqandi had neither slumbered nor fallen asleep, nor given rest to his eyes, and the whole people of the Muslims was on his side. They gave a bribe, not a small one, to the emirs, both great and small, and to the armies, and what is said was fulfilled: "The bribe blinds the eyes of the wise in judgment."[315]

They turned away from the covenant and agreement. The metropolitan was secretly captured and delivered to Toghan, so he might go make the *catholicos* and the Christians come down from the citadel, and otherwise he would be killed without pity. They took him outside of the city at night, to a nearby mountain, while no one noticed at all. The suffering of all the Christians there increased, of all confessions, who had gathered in the city, and all the boys from the [metropolitan's] residence fled and scattered. No helper or guardian remained, save from the venerable mercy of God, who acts in accordance with his kindness and administers things in accordance with his mercy.

The metropolitan had a younger brother who fled and went to the emir Chupan (may he be preserved in life) and told him what had been done, saying, "The servant of the emir of emirs, the metropolitan who came to him yesterday concerning the citadel of Arbil, has been taken to Arbil by deceit and by force!" The emir became very angry, and he sent a messenger and brought back the metropolitan from the hands of the cruel men. He brought him in front of the victorious king, and the metropolitan again repeated his speech about the *catholicos* and the Christians. The king commanded for the *catholicos* to be brought to the camp, and

315. Deuteronomy 16:19.

for the Christians to come down from the citadel and not to be harmed. The king summoned Toghan and admonished him about these things, ordering him to go to Arbil.

As for the metropolitan, the great emir of emirs and head of the *dīwān*, Chupan, had him brought to his own house. He wrote several letters on his behalf to all the Mongol emirs who had gone to besiege the citadel, and to the emir Chechäk, son-in-law of the late King Hülegü,[316] the father of all these kings, for them to bring down the *catholicos* with honor, in accordance with the royal decree, and to bring down the Christians without causing them any harm. He entrusted to the messenger, "If anyone lays a hand on the Christians, do not bring them down." He sent the metropolitan with honor and entrusted to the king's messenger: "If the Muslims or the Kurds do not obey, stay with the *catholicos* and the Christians and send someone to inform me."

The metropolitan came with the messenger first to the emir Chechäk, and they showed the stipulation of the emir of emirs Chupan. He and his wife rejoiced at the rescue of the *catholicos* and the Christians, and the emir Chechäk sent a hundred other Mongol horsemen of his, who went to the citadel to help with this action. He also wrote to the eight hundred Kurdish infantrymen under his command for them to bring down the *catholicos*.

But Toghan, three days before the arrival of the metropolitan and the messenger with him, had arrived and sent to the *catholicos* and showed him the decree for him to come down. Without hesitation he came down, on Friday, June 26, [1310,] with the bishops and priests who were with him. He obeyed the decree.

Toghan persuaded him to go up again to the citadel and bring down the Christians. With a simple heart, he went up and commanded

---

316. Hülegü (d. 1265) founded the Ilkhanate dynasty. His fourth daughter Tödögäch was first married to a member of the Oirat tribe named Tänggiz. When a Mongol man died, his widows would be provided for by marrying them to their stepsons, brothers-in-law, or other male relatives of their deceased husband (though never to their own sons), so after Tänggiz died, Tödögäch married his son Sülämish, and after he died, she married Sülämish's son Chechäk.

them to come down. Those poor people innocently obeyed the royal and fatherly command, and on Saturday morning they came down with their sons, their daughters, and their wives, about 150 men more or less, not counting the women and children, with no weapon, no sword, and no knife.

When the evil people of the Muslims saw them come down, they became bitter and angry. They drew their swords and butchered them, great and small, without pity and without fear, and they captured the women and children. They acted on the pretext that someone had shot arrows at them from the citadel, but all of this was in order to terrify the *catholicos*, so that he would not come down, so that what was spoken about him in the king's presence would be confirmed, so that the king might become angry and give a command, and he would be killed, he and all the Christians.

The *catholicos*, hoping in Christ, began to come down while weeping and groaning with a bitter heart. He considered the swords insignificant, because he thought, "If I die of hunger in the citadel, I would be called by the name of rebels, and this would be a great evil. It would be better for me to obey to the point of death and go down. If my Lord saves me, it is a triumph for me, and if not, I am ready to receive the crown of martyrdom in the name of Christ."

The Christians fell at his feet, crying and saying, "We will not allow you to go down," and so did the bishops who were with him, but he replied, "There is no way for me to avoid going down; however, I will not at all force anyone to come down with me. The one who wishes to share in my sufferings, I will not hinder."

He departed from them, and there joined him three bishops who were with him, the boys from the [patriarchal] residence, and some monks and priests. They went down along the wall, walking on the murdered and slaughtered ones who had sought refuge without sin. The *catholicos* was looking at his children with their bellies torn open, their guts thrown on the ground, and there was no one to bury them or prepare them for burial. He followed Toghan's words, thinking that he was a friend, when in reality he was a friend of betrayal.

Then with the prophet the *catholicos* said in his heart,[317]
I called to my lovers, but they deceived me.
My priests and my elders perished within me,[318]
Who searched for food to save their lives, but they did not find any.
See, Lord, that I am very distressed and my insides are disturbed.
My heart is upset within me, because I have become very bitter.
Outside the sword has destroyed, and what is in the house is death.
Hear that I am sighing, and there is none to comfort me.
All my enemies heard of my calamity and rejoiced at what you have done to me.
Bring the day that you have called, when they will be like me.
Let all the evil—of the Hagarenes—come before you!
Strike them as you have struck me for all my sins—
And you have made me known among my children and my dear ones—
For my sighs are many, and my heart is wretched.[319]

What happened then? Toghan came to the *catholicos* laughing, like someone who has done nothing. He brought the *catholicos* to his tent, honored him, and gave him a cup while kneeling on his knees. The *catholicos* said to him, "Is this what you promised? Is this what the royal decree said that you read to us yesterday, in which it was ordered that everyone who comes down should not be harmed, and their noses should not be caused to bleed?" He replied, "They shot arrows from the citadel and hit two men who died!" The *catholicos* replied, "Those who shot the arrows would

317. The book of Lamentations is ascribed to the prophet Jeremiah.

318. I.e., within Jerusalem; this section is spoken in the voice of Jerusalem personified.

319. Lamentations 1:19–22, with the insertion of "the Hagarenes" and the second-to-last line.

rightly have been executed, not these who obeyed the royal decree and came down!" Toghan remained silent and did not answer a word.

Although the cursed peoples took counsel how to destroy the *catholicos*, Toghan and Nasir, Dilqandi's brother, acted as if they had no knowledge, so that they might have a defense, but the Lord delights in his chosen ones and sends them salvation from a place they do not know and do not perceive.

The metropolitan considered and said to the emir Chechäk, "Emir, you know what kind of man Toghan is. He preceded us to Arbil and I am afraid that he will do some evil before we arrive. It would be good if the emir sends one of his men and one of the companions of the messenger who is with me."

He did this without delay, sending a man with one of those who were accompanying the messenger. He arrived in Arbil that same Saturday, toward evening, after those oppressed people had been killed. They went to greet the *catholicos* and Toghan, and they showed him the copy that the emir of emirs Chupan wrote at the king's command concerning the *catholicos*.

Upon hearing this, the appearance of their faces, Toghan's own and that of Nasir, was troubled and turned pale, and they began whispering to each other, but they had no trick left, since the men who had come saw the *catholicos*. As it grew dark, Nasir and Toghan rode with him for a mile, and he continued on to the village of ʿAmkava.[320]

The metropolitan and the messenger with him arrived on the morning of Sunday, June 27,[321] and saw what had happened, and it pained them and their grief grew. They were a little relieved by the rescue of the *catholicos* and the bishops who were with him. They immediately went to the *catholicos* and made known to him the words of the great emir and the

---

320. This village, now called ʿAnkawa, is today a suburb of Erbil in Iraqi Kurdistan.

321. In 1310, June 27 was a Saturday, which was just described, so this should read Sunday, June 28.

contents of the royal decree concerning him.[322] The *catholicos* rejoiced and blessed them and the emir.

The next morning [Monday, June 29], the messenger went to Toghan and asked to go up to the citadel. He would not allow him: "They will kill you! They are *yāghīs*!" The messenger said, "Whether they kill me or not, I will go up to them!" When he went up, Toghan did not allow him to bring any food or drink with him: "You have come here to save the Christians, who hate our religion and are the enemies of our people. Since the Christians did not obey the king's commands, neither will we obey your emir's command!"

The messenger did not pay attention, but he went up to the citadel and showed them the emir's stipulation, and they agreed to come down and all of them obeyed.

The messenger went down at evening, and he brought down three people with him: one of them they snatched from him and killed, and the others were taken captive. He brought with him the keys to the citadel, which he handed to Toghan. He sadly came to the *catholicos*, and they took counsel about what he should do. "The people below are many and strong. In the citadel there is no food even for a day, and they prevent me from bringing up any, and those whom I bring down, they seize and kill. I have no helper here, and I do not know what to do, but I will gather the men who came with me and these hundred horsemen of the emir Chechäk. They will bring down the women and children first, and escort them to the villages. As for the men who make war, at night they and I, and the men with me, will cross and escape, and if anyone raises a hand against us, we will do the same!" The *catholicos* said, "You know what is best; do what God grants you."

On Tuesday [June 30], the messenger went up to them, gathered them around him, and spoke with them. Most of them listened to his advice, but as the proverb says, "From the thigh a worm comes out,"[323] some of the citadel's inhabitants had already betrayed the rest and had

322. The "great emir" in this sentence is again Chupan.

323. This proverb is not attested elsewhere and is obscure in meaning.

allied themselves with Nasir al-Din,[324] and every day they were sending word and informing him of all that took place in the citadel. When they saw that the people had taken counsel to go down, they went and informed him. Nasir wrote at once, "The inhabitants of the citadel, apart from the mountaineers, will not owe anything to anybody and will not have to come down from the citadel, but their hearts should be at ease. The mountaineers will pay the messengers' expenses, and if they desire, they can come down."

The people of the citadel were divided from one another by this message: some went down to him with their families and were not harmed. They were allowed to come to the village of ʿAmkava, but on the following day they came, took them from there, and they were killed.

From then on, there remained in the citadel no chief, no leader, no one giving advice, and no one knowledgeable. The messenger alone remained in the residence of the *catholicos*, and then he went down and left them without assistance with bitter tears and loud moans. Alas for the hour full of losses! Alas for the grievous time that brings griefs! If they were staying, no one had the strength even to draw some water. And who could face a battle?

Starvation fully destroyed them. Wheat had already run out, and a pound was sold for eight *zūzē*. As for salt, who could find it? Donkeys, dogs, cats had all been eaten already. Old leather they had not left. They filled up on pips, that is, seeds of cotton. Widows stretched out their hands, weeping, and there was no one to bind up the fracture. Anyone to prepare the dead for burial, there was not at all. Who had the strength to dig graves? Who could feel pity and show mercy? Who could give alms? Orphans died on dung piles, others fell in their houses and shriveled up, and others threw themselves from the walls and those below welcomed them with their swords, cutting them to pieces.

Oh, for the honored ones whom the Lord despised! Oh, for the honorable ones whom God has rejected! Oh, for the people for whom there remains no atonement and no one to bring help to them! See,

324. This seems to be a variant name for Nasir.

hearers, how severe is the punishment of our Lord for those who do not repent! How hard is your staff, our God! How harmful is your strike, our Guardian! How bitter are your torments, our Physician! You turned away your face, the crown fell from their head, and their joy turned to grief. They wept day and night, their tears ran down their cheeks, and they had no comforter among all their friends. All groan and seek bread, their eyes are dark with tears, and their insides are disturbed. Their honor has been thrown to the ground by the breaking of their citadel. The children and toddlers ask their mothers, "Where is bread? Where is oil?" while shaken like the slain before them. "They ask for bread and there is no one who breaks some and gives it to them. Those who ate delicacies are now thrown into the streets, and those who were raised in purple robes now sleep on piles of dung."[325] "Their appearance is darker than coals and they are unrecognizable. Their skin shrank over their bones. They dried up and became like wood. Those killed by the sword were better than those killed by starvation. Women ate their offspring, and the hands of the compassionate women boiled their own children, and they became food for them."[326] "Children and old men lay on the ground, virgins and youths"[327] were abused, men were butchered, and the Lord did not have pity on them. Arrows entered into their kidneys and they became a laughingstock among all the peoples,[328] because "the Lord accomplished his wrath, and he poured out the wrath of his anger,"[329] because "in vain their sentinels stood watch."[330] Henceforth with the prophet they are crying out, saying:

325. Lamentations 4:4–5.

326. Lamentations 4:8–10.

327. Lamentations 2:21.

328. Cf. Lamentations 3:13–14.

329. Lamentations 4:11.

330. Lamentations 4:16.

Our sins have awoken against us, and our strength has become weak.
The Lord has delivered us into the hand of one whose strength we cannot overcome.[331]
Righteous is the Lord, whom we have provoked!
Listen, all peoples, and see our pain!
Our virgins and our youths have gone into captivity.[332]
Our youths and men have been killed.
What can we say? That our priests led us astray, and did not reveal to us our sins?[333]
Far from it! They persuaded and we did not listen,
    and they rebuked and we did not pay attention.
We despised them, and we did not favor them.
We had no mercy for our elders and we oppressed the widows.
We persecuted the poor.
Our wickedness is greater than Jerusalem's,
    and our evil surpassed that in the days of Noah.
For this reason, the Lord did what he had planned,
And he fulfilled his word, as he commanded in the days of old.
He overthrew us and did not spare us.
He made our enemies surround us and raised up the horn of those afflicting us.
All our enemies opened their mouths against us, they hissed and gnashed their teeth.[334]
They sold our children far away, abused our virgins in front of us,
    and raped our wives before our eyes, while saying,
"We will devour you! This is the day we waited for!
We have found it and we have seen it!"[335]

331. Cf. Lamentations 1:14.

332. Cf. Lamentations 1:18.

333. Cf. Lamentations 2:14.

334. Cf. Lamentations 2:16–17.

335. Cf. Lamentations 2:17.

The Muslim people then went up to the citadel with Toghan and Nasir, on Wednesday, July 1 in that year, 1621 of the Greeks [1310], and overpowered it. They killed everyone they found and they spared no one. They took captive all whom they saw. They looted the treasures and plundered the riches. Those left from the *qāyājīs* they threw down from the top of the wall, and those below welcomed them with swords until they finished them. They sold most of the women and virgins, and they were giving them to all who came to them, presenting them like gifts to them. In short, they brought into the open all the evil that was hidden in their hearts.

We too, with that same prophet, say: Rejoice, people of Arbil, since the cup also shall come to you! You shall mourn and be disturbed,[336] and no one will save you, because the Lord remembers what happened to his people and how his inheritance was looted. "The Lord is good to anyone who hopes in him and to the soul that seeks him."[337] May he turn back to you your retribution according to the deeds of your hands. May he give you sorrow of heart, and may his striking chase you. May he destroy you in his anger and wipe you out from under the sky, since you demolished his churches and tore to pieces the sheep of his flock.[338] And all those who pass along the road shall clap their hands at you, whistle, shake their heads, and say, "This is Arbil, which the Lord has cursed!"

The Death of Mar Yahballaha

The *catholicos*, with the Mongols and the bishops who were with him, [the Mongols] who had come from the emir Chechäk to conduct him, went to the village of Beth Sayyade, but with much fear, and with trembling, great sorrow, and grief. They remained a few days there, until

336. Cf. Lamentations 4:21. "The cup" refers to God's judgment.

337. Lamentations 3:25.

338. Referring to God's people as "his flock" or "his sheep" is a metaphor common in the Bible.

they had gathered some gold, which they gave to the messenger of the emir Chupan, the hundred men who came from the emir Chechäk, and the Kurds who were with them. Then they left and went to the [royal] camp.

On July 8 of that year [1310] the *catholicos* arrived before the queen, the emir Chechäk's wife. She honored him greatly, and also sent men to the camp with him.

As soon as he arrived, he went to the great emir Chupan, and he saw him and honored him as was right. From there he entered the city, and all the emirs were informed about him. He entered before the victorious king, blessed him according to the custom, and put the cup into his hands. The king in turn gave him the cup, but neither of them spoke a word to the other. The *catholicos* went out from there grieved. He had decided that if the king questioned him, he would make known to him all that had happened to him, and also to his flock. His heart was very broken by this, and he stayed there for a whole month, hoping that perhaps something might be restored or that someone would ask him about what had happened.

Once some of the necessary business for the patriarchal residence and the Christians were completed, he returned to the monastery he had built beside Maragha, and he resolved in his heart that he would never again visit the [royal] camp: "I am tired of serving the Mongols."

The *catholicos* spent the winter of the Greek year 1622 [1310–11] in that monastery. In the summer he went to Tabriz because he had heard that the emir Irinjin (may our Lord preserve his life) would arrive at Tabriz, and when he came, he met him at once, and he honored the *catholicos* greatly. He offered him presents and gifts, as did his wife, the daughter of King Ahmad, son of the late King Hülegü.[339] She was honored in the kingdom because the victorious king had married her daughter, and she was his chief wife at the time. The emir Irinjin and his wife

339. Tegüder Ahmad's daughter Könchäk married Irinjin, the son of Sarucha Agha, and their daughter Qutlughshah married Öljeitü in 1305. Irinjin was also the brother of Öljeitü's mother Örüg Khatun.

gave the *catholicos* the sum of 10,000 *dīnār*s, which is 60,000 *zūzē*, and horses for riding. The emir also gave a large village to the church of Saint Shallita the holy martyr, for in it his deceased father was buried, and so were his mother and wives.[340]

The *catholicos* spent the winter of the Greek year 1623 [1311–12] in that monastery, and the following summer as well. When his situation became known to the king through some counselors, he granted him 5,000 *dīnār*s, and they brought to him his food every year. The king also gave him villages in the Baghdad region.

The metropolitan fathers and bishops whom he ordained for the flocks by laying hands on them are, as of this year, seventy-five.[341] This is the state of things.

He lived in that monastery that he had built until the Greek year 1629 [1317–18]. He passed away on the night of the Sunday of the hymn *mā shbiḥ mashknak*, November 15 [1317].[342] He was buried in the monastery that he built. May his memory be a blessing.

May the prayers of Mar Yahballaha the *catholicos* and of Rabban Sawma be for us, for the entire world to its end, and for the holy Church and her children. To God be glory, honor, thanksgiving, and worship, forever and ever. Amen and amen.

---

340. Giving a village to the church means that the profits from that village's agriculture will support the church economically. It was not common for Mongols to be buried in churches, but Irinjin's father Sarucha was the brother of Hülegü's queen Doquz Khatun. Irinjin's mother and the other wives who were buried there are not identified.

341. The Christian ritual of ordination involved the patriarch laying his hands on the bishop being ordained.

342. That Sunday was in fact November 13, not November 15. Since days were counted as starting at sundown, "the night of" refers to the night before, which we would count as late on November 12.

Glossary

archdeacon a deacon responsible for leading other deacons or for administering a bishop's residence

asceticism a general term for various forms of physical self-discipline for spiritual gain, such as fasting from food; someone who practices asceticism is an ascetic

basileus a Greek title for the Byzantine emperor

bishop a church leader responsible for a region

cardinals clergy in and near Rome with special functions in running the papacy, including selecting the new pope

catholicos the title of the patriarch of the Church of the East, indicating his authority over all other bishops

cell within a monastery, the dwelling place of a monk, bishop, metropolitan, or *catholicos*

clappers wooden or metal sounding board used by Middle Eastern Christians in a way similar to Western church bells

deacon a lower rank of clergy who assists in church services and some practical needs of the churches

dīnār a coin, made of silver or gold, worth six *dirham*s in the Ilkhanate

dirham a silver coin, worth 1/6 of a *dīnār*

diocese the region over which a bishop has authority

dīwān the government bureaucracy

emir an Arabic term for a commander or military leader

farsakh a unit of distance, about 3.5 miles long

habit the outfit which distinguished monks or nuns from lay Christians

Hagarenes a derogatory term for Muslims, derived from the traditional idea that Arabs are descended from Ishmael, the son of Abraham and Hagar in the Bible

jizya an individual tax required from non-Muslims under Muslim rule

khaghan see *qa'an*

khan a Mongol title for a ruler

khatun a Mongol title for queen

khwāja a Persian title of respect

Mar a title of honor used for bishops, patriarchs, and saints, meaning "my lord"

metropolitan a rank of bishop in eastern churches corresponding to a western archbishop, with authority over other bishops

mithqal a measurement of weight, about 4.5 grams

monasticism the practice of living as a monk, or the institution of monks living together

monk an individual who has dedicated their life to a particular religious lifestyle, typically including self-discipline and celibacy

paiza a metal tablet conferred by a khan that grants certain standard privileges to the person who carries it; there were different varieties of *paiza*s, made of different metals and having various images depicted on them, which corresponded to different levels of privileges

patriarch a church official who is highest in his own church hierarchy, not subject to other clergy

phakialion a Greek term, typically used in Syriac to describe a special type of cloak worn by Eastern Syriac bishops, but in this text describing a mantle associated with Jesus's mother, Saint Mary

qa'an a Mongol title for the "great khan" (also spelled *khaghan*)

qāḍī an Islamic judge

qāshānī a style of decorative glazed tiles or tilework

qāyājīs soldiers trained to fight in mountains, in service of the Mongols, including many Christians (such as Georgians and Armenians)

qnōmē a technical Syriac term that roughly corresponds to *hypostasis* in Aristotelian philosophy; the Church of the East uses the term to refer to both the three "Persons" of the Trinity and also the two "instantiated natures" of the incarnate Christ

relics physical objects, including body parts or possessions, associated with a dead saint

reliquary a container for holding relics

sacristy a side room in which the special vestments for the liturgy were stored

sukur a kind of parasol or umbrella held over the head of someone to be honored

sunqur a golden *paiza* decorated with a falcon, which granted particular privileges

tagavor the Armenian word for "king"

tamgha an official seal applied to documents, and thus by implication a document to which the seal has been applied

tonsure a ritual head-shaving that marks monks

vestments special clothes worn for church services

vizier the leader of the government bureaucracy under a ruler, a high-ranking position responsible for advising the ruler and making the government follow his orders

waqf an endowment, especially for a religious institution

yāghī a Turkish word describing someone who has not submitted to the Mongol ruler and therefore is considered in a state of rebellion

yarligh the Mongol word for "edicts" or "decrees," which were often granted to recognize a lesser authority and grant privileges

zūzē a general Syriac term for coins, in this text typically used for silver *dirhams*

Select Bibliography

Overviews

Baum, Wilhelm, and Dietmar Winkler. *The Church of the East: A Concise History*. London: RoutledgeCurzon, 2003.

Baumer, Christoph. *The Church of the East: An Illustrated History of Assyrian Christianity*. New ed. London: I. B. Tauris, 2016.

Biran, Michal. *Qaidu and the Rise of the Independent Mongol State in Central Asia*. Surrey, U.K.: Curzon, 1997.

Jackson, Peter. *The Mongols and the Islamic World: From Conquest to Conversion*. New Haven, Conn.: Yale University Press, 2017.

Jackson, Peter. *The Mongols and the West, 1221–1410*. 2nd ed. London: Routledge, 2018.

May, Timothy. *The Mongol Empire*. Edinburgh: Edinburgh University Press, 2018.

Morgan, David. *The Mongols*. 2nd ed. Malden, Mass.: Blackwell, 2007.

Murre-van den Berg, Heleen. "The Church of the East in Mesopotamia in the Mongol Period." In Roman Malek with Peter Hofrichter, eds., *Jingjiao: The Church of the East in China and Central Asia*, 377–94. Sankt Augustin: Institut Monumenta Serica, 2006.

Primary Sources

Atwood, Christopher F. *The Rise of the Mongols: Five Chinese Sources*. Indianapolis: Hackett Publishing Company, 2021.

Bar Hebraeus, Gregory. *The Ecclesiastical Chronicle: An English Translation*. Translated by David Wilmshurst. Piscataway, N.J.: Gorgias Press, 2016.

Bar Hebraeus, Gregory. *The Chronography of Gregory Abû'l Faraj, the Son of Aaron, the Hebrew Physician, Commonly Known as Bar Hebraeus*. Translated by E. A. Wallis Budge. London: Oxford University Press, 1932.

Borbone, Pier Giorgio. *The History of Mar Yahballaha and Rabban Sauma.* Translated by Laura E. Parodi. Hamburg: Tredition Verlag, 2021.

Bottini, Laura E. "Due lettere inedite del patriarca mar Yahballaha III (1281–1317)." *Rivista degli studi orientali* (1992): 239–56.

Lamy, Thomas J., ed. *Sancti Ephraem Syri Hymni et sermones*, vol. 3. Mechelen, Belgium: H. Dessain, 1889.

Rashid al-Din Fazlullah. *Jami`u't-Tawarikh: Compendium of Chronicles*. Translated by W. M. Thackston. Cambridge, Mass.: Harvard University Press, 1999.

Riccoldo da Montecroce. "The Book of Pilgrimage." In Rita George-Tvrtković, ed., *A Christian Pilgrim in Medieval Iraq: Riccoldo da Montecroce's Encounter with Islam*, 175–227. Turnhout, Belgium: Brepols, 2012.

Ṣalībā Ibn Yūḥannā al-Mawṣilī. *Asfār al-asrār III: Livre cinquième*. Edited by Gianmaria Gianazza. Beirut: Éditions du CEDRAC, 2024.

Teule, Herman G. B. "The Synod of Timotheos II—1318." In Alberto Melloni and Ephrem Ishac, eds., *The General Councils of the Eastern Christian Churches*, 2:1443–79. Turnhout, Belgium: Brepols, 2023.

William of Rubruck. *The Mission of Friar William of Rubruck: His Journey to the Court of the Great Khan Möngke, 1253–1255.* Translated by Peter Jackson. London: Hakluyt Society, 1990; Indianapolis: Hackett Publishing Company, 2009.

Winkler, Dietmar W. "Two Letters of Yahballaha III to the Popes of Rome: Historical Context and English Translation." In Li Tang and Dietmar W. Winkler, eds., *Artifact, Text, Context: Studies on Syriac Christianity in China and Central Asia*, 213–28. Münster: LIT Verlag, 2020.

Selected Detailed Studies

Amitai, Reuven. "Edward of England and Abagha Ilkhan: A Reexamination of a Failed Attempt at Mongol-Frankish Cooperation." In Michael Gervers and James M. Powell, eds., *Tolerance and Intolerance: Social Conflict in the Age of the Crusades*, 75–82. Syracuse, N.Y.: Syracuse University Press, 2001.

Broadbridge, Anne. *Women and the Making of the Mongol Empire*. Cambridge: Cambridge University Press, 2018.

De Nicola, Bruno. *Women in Mongol Iran: The Khātūns, 1206–1335*. Edinburgh: Edinburgh University Press, 2017.

Dickens, Mark. "Yahbalaha the Turk: An Inner Asian Patriarch of the Eastern Christians." In Mark Dickens, ed., *Echoes of a Forgotten Presence: Reconstructing the History of the Church of the East in Central Asia*, 272–92. Münster: LIT Verlag, 2020.

Foltz, Richard. "Ecumenical Mischief under the Mongols." *Central Asiatic Journal* 43, no. 1 (1999): 42–68.

Ho, Colleen C. "Rabban Ṣauma: A Medieval Shape Shifter." In Lily Anne Y. Welty Tamai, Ingrid Dineen-Wimberly, and Paul Spickard, eds., *Shape Shifters: Journeys across Terrains of Race and Identity*, 83–101. Lincoln: University of Nebraska Press, 2020.

Jackson, Peter. "The Mongols and the Faith of the Conquered." In Reuven Amitai and Michal Biran, eds., *Mongols, Turks, and Others: Eurasian Nomads and the Sedentary World*, 245–90. Leiden: Brill, 2005.

Kamola, Stefan. *Making Mongol History: Rashid al-Din and the Jamiʿ al-Tawarikh*. Edinburgh: Edinburgh University Press, 2019.

Maraini, Fosco. "Per amor di Gerusalemme: Due cristiani dalla Mongolia a Bordeaux." *L'indice dei libri del mese* 18 (2001): 13.

Melville, Charles. "Abū Saʿīd and the Revolt of the Amirs in 1319." In Denise Aigle, ed., *L'Iran face a la domination mongole*, 89–120. Tehran: Institut français de recherche en Iran, 1997.

Pfeiffer, Judith. "Aḥmad Tegüder's Second Letter to Qalā'ūn (682/1283)." In Judith Pfeiffer and Sholeh A. Quinn, eds., *History and Historiography of Post-Mongol Central Asia and the Middle East: Studies in Honor of John E. Woods*, 167–202. Wiesbaden: Harrassowitz, 2006.

Romano, John F. "The Travelogue of Rabban Sauma as a Source for Thirteenth-Century Liturgy." *Archiv für Liturgie-wissenschaft* 58/59 (2016/17): 59–101.

Rossabi, Morris. *Khubilai Khan: His Life and Times*. Berkeley: University of California Press, 1988.

Tannous, Jack B. V. *The Making of the Medieval Middle East: Religion, Society, and Simple Believers*. Princeton, N.J.: Princeton University Press, 2020.

Image Credits

Unless otherwise noted below, all images are in the public domain.

Image 2 (Golden Paiza): UN Photo/Andrea Brizzi.

Image 4 (Stromboli): David Yoon.

Image 5 (Basilica of St. Denis): Diliff (https://commons.wikimedia.org/wiki/File:Basilica_of_Saint_Denis_North_Transept_Rose_Window,_Paris,_France_-_Diliff.jpg), "Basilica of Saint Denis North Transept Rose Window, Paris, France – Diliff," https://creativecommons.org/licenses/by-sa/3.0/legalcode

Image 11 (Arbil Citadel): Osama Shukir Muhammed Amin FRCP(Glasg) (https://commons.wikimedia.org/wiki/File:49._Erbil_Citadel,_Erbil_Governorate,_Iraqi_Kurdistan.jpg), https://creativecommons.org/licenses/by-sa/4.0/legalcode

Image 12 (Öljeitü's Mausoleum): Farzad Yousefian (https://commons.wikimedia.org/wiki/File:Gonbad_Soltaniye.jpg), https://creativecommons.org/licenses/by-sa/4.0/legalcode

Index

Abaqa, 5–6, 19, 24, 51, 56–59, 61, 93
Abgar of Edessa, 73
Abraham (biblical patriarch), 38, 59n82, 90, 108n238, 154
Addai, 9, 70, 115
Ahmad Tegüder, 6, 19, 59–62, 151
Ala Tagh, 91, 94, 108–9
'Amkava, 145, 147
Andronikos II, 64–65, 67
Ani, 51
Aragon, 68–69
Arbil, 15–17, 21–26, 29, 50, 57, 93, 102, 106–8, 110, 112–14, 115n250, 117, 120, 122–26, 129–132, 134, 136, 137n306, 138, 140–42, 145, 150
Arghun, 6–8, 19–20, 59, 61–64, 67, 69, 71, 73, 76–77, 80–83, 87–90, 91n191, 92, 95, 105, 121, 139
Armenians, 12, 15, 97, 107n233, 124n273, 131
Ashnukh. *See* Ushnuviya
Ay Buqa, 46
Azerbaijan, 49, 56, 58, 94, 98n212, 112, 116, 118, 123

Baghdad, 1, 4, 9–11, 14, 19–20, 27, 44n33, 49–50, 54–55, 57–58, 61, 70, 93–94, 95n203, 100, 102–4, 106, 110–11, 117–18, 132, 152
Baidu, 7, 20, 92–95, 106n231
Balu. *See* Zayn al-Din Balu
Beijing. *See* Khanbaliq
Beth Garmai, 50, 58
Beth Sayyade, 132, 134, 137, 150
Boraqchin Egächi, 106
Bordeaux, 80
Buddhists, 20, 91n192

cardinals, 13, 27, 69–73, 75–76, 82, 84, 86, 153
Chaghatai Khanate, 5, 8, 19, 53n63
Charles of Anjou, 68–69
Chechäk, 142, 145–46, 150–51
Chinggis Khan. *See* Genghis Khan
Choban. *See* Chupan
Christmas, 30, 99, 117
Chupan, 8–9, 17, 24, 29, 140–42, 145, 146n322, 151
Constantine, 66–67, 69n113, 75, 108n236
Constantinople, 1, 12, 27, 64–67, 79n149, 80
Court of the Romans, 20, 93, 118
Ctesiphon, 9, 27, 55, 57

Damascus, 4, 119
Denha I, 18–19, 49, 51, 53–57, 103
dīnārs, 41, 58, 91–92, 97, 99–102, 111, 116, 152–53

dirhams, 58, 92, 153, 155
dīwān, 59, 103, 110–11, 119, 142, 153
Diyar Bakr, 94, 120, 127, 135n303
Doquz Khatun, 4–5, 13, 91, 103, 152n340
dragon, 67

Easter, 18, 20, 22, 31, 39n10, 58n78, 75n133, 84n167, 86, 94, 100, 120
Edessa, 9, 70n116, 73
Edward I of England, 5, 79–81
England, 1, 3, 5, 9, 19, 79–80
Ephrem, 96, 102n221
Epiphany, 93, 118
Erbil. *See* Arbil
Esen Qutlugh, 133, 139
Etna. *See* Mount Etna
Eusebius of Nicomedia, 67n106

Feast of the Cross (*shkhāḥtā*), 31, 108, 116
Forty Martyrs, 92, 115
France, 1, 8, 19, 76–77, 79, 80n152, 87
Francis. *See* Philip IV of France
Franks, 5–7, 19, 63, 67, 69, 76n137, 81, 88, 110, 115

Gascony, 80, 81n156
Gazarta of Beth Zabdai, 50
Geikhatu, 7, 9, 20, 90–92, 94–95, 99
Genghis Khan, 2–4, 13, 18
Genoa, 19, 76, 81
George, Saint (martyr), 92, 105, 115
Georgia, 51
Germans, 81
Ghazan, 7–8, 15–16, 20–21, 24–25, 59n82, 95, 98, 100–104, 106–14, 117–21, 128, 139n308

Hagia Sophia, 65–66
Hajji Dilqandi, 17, 127, 129, 133–34, 136, 138, 141, 145
Hamadan, 93n198, 102, 106, 110, 137
Het'um II, 97–98
Hilla, 21, 118
Honorius IV, 69
Hoqu, 47
Hülegü, 4–5, 7, 13, 59, 91n194, 95n203, 102–3, 106n231, 127n283, 142, 151, 152n340

Indians, 38
Irinjin, 24, 122, 151–52
Irinjin Torji. *See* Geikhatu
Ishoʿsabran (d. 610), 115, 131
Italy, 67–68, 76n142, 77n143

"Jacobites," 12, 131
Jaghatu, 106, 123
James II of Aragon, 68
James the Dismembered, 92, 115
Jeremiah, 42, 144
Jerusalem, 1, 4–5, 18, 24, 25n15, 27, 44, 46–47, 49, 51–52, 56, 58, 70–71, 73n124, 75–77, 80, 82, 93, 108n236, 144n318, 149
jizya, 15, 101, 111, 123–24, 154
John Chrysostom, 66–67
John the Baptist, 65, 75–76, 84, 94, 113–15

Kashan. *See* Qashan
Kashgar, 48
Khanbaliq, 39, 49
Khorasan, 7, 48, 60–61, 107–8, 121
Khotan, 47
Kokhe, 9–10, 50, 57
Könchäk, 151
Kosheng, 18, 43, 45, 46n36
Kun Buqa, 46
Kurdistan, 16, 145n320
Kurds, 106–7, 114, 131, 135–36, 140, 142, 151

Lateran palace, 69n113, 85n171
lawyers, 55, 125
Lent, 18, 31, 58, 76–77, 83, 104, 107, 108n236, 118, 128
Lombardy, 76
Lord's Fast. *See* Lent

Makkika II, 102–3
Maʿnyo, 115, 131
Maragha, 10, 20–21, 27, 49, 61, 63, 90, 92, 94–95, 97–98, 103–4, 106, 110, 112–14, 116, 118, 120, 151
Mardin, 50, 120n262
Mari, 9–10, 50, 70, 92, 115
Mary, mother of Jesus, 3, 61, 65–66, 71–72, 75, 86–87, 91, 115, 131, 154
Mary Magdalene, 65
Michael of Tarʿel, 50, 53, 55, 128–29
mithqal, 64, 88, 154
Möngke, 4, 105
Mongolian new year. *See* White Feast
Mosul, 23, 50, 58–59, 102, 112–13, 133
Mount Etna, 67n107
Mughan, 98, 100, 112, 117, 124

Najm al-Din Ghazi of Mardin, 120
Naples, 68
Nasir Dilqandi, 17, 125, 127, 129–30, 134, 135n301, 145, 147, 150
Nawruz, 7, 15–16, 20, 29, 95, 97–100, 103–4, 107–8
Nebuchadnezzar, 118
Nicaea, Council of, 66
Nicholas IV, 6, 20, 27–28, 70, 82–88, 90n189
Nineveh, 58, 108n236
Nisibis, 50

Old Saint Peter's Basilica, 69, 73
Öljeitü, 6, 8–9, 15–17, 20–21, 24, 90n189, 121–25, 127–28, 133, 135–43, 145–46, 151–52
Önggüd, 13, 18–19, 46n36, 53n62
Örüg Khatun, 121, 122n266, 139, 151n339

paiza, 56–57, 60–61, 64, 92, 117, 154–55
Palestine, 5, 63, 71, 112, 118, 135
Palestinians, 140
Palm Sunday, 83
Paris, 2, 19, 77–80
Passover, 75n133, 76, 84n167
Paul, 9, 32, 42, 69, 73–74, 115
Pentecost, 31, 44n32, 120
Persian, 22–23, 56, 76n137, 88, 109n241, 119, 123, 154

Peter, 9, 22n11, 66, 69, 73, 75, 115
Petition of the Ninevites, 31, 108
phakialion, 87, 115, 154
Philip IV of France, 77–80, 87
pope, 1–2, 6, 11, 19–20, 25, 27–28, 64, 67, 69–71, 73–76, 81–88, 105, 119, 153

Qaidu, 4, 48
Qashan, 115n249, 119
qāyājīs, 15–17, 107, 124, 126, 128–29, 140–41, 147, 150, 155
Qazvin, 121n263, 123
Qubilai, 4–5, 13, 18, 25n15, 46–47, 48n43, 59–60
Qutlughshah (Mongol general), 108
Qutlughshah (wife of Öljeitü), 151
Qutui Khatun, 61

Ramadan, 103
Rashid al-Din Hamadani, 5, 7, 108n237, 109, 121n263, 139
relics, 22, 50, 65–66, 73–77, 79–80, 86–87, 92, 114–15, 119
Rogation of the Ninevites. *See* Petition of the Ninevites
running water, 114

Sacro Catino, 76
Saʿd al-Din Sawaji, 139
Sahand, 121
Saint John Lateran, 75, 84, 85
Saint Mary Church in Urmia, 61
Saint Paul Outside the Walls, 74
Saint-Denis, 78
Sainte-Chapelle, 79
Samarkand, 58
San Lorenzo Church in Genoa, 76
San Paolo alle Tre Fontane, 74
Santa Croce in Gerusalemme, 85
Santa Francesca Romana, 75
Santa Maria Maggiore, 75, 86
Santi Apostoli, 75
Sati Beg (Mongol commander), 129
Sati Beg (sister of Abu Saʿid), 8, 129n288
scribes, 31, 37n1, 43n26, 55, 59–60, 106, 125, 127, 139
Sea of the Dragon. *See* Tyrrhenian Sea
Seleucia, 27, 55, 57
Shahrazur, 93
Shallita, 63, 97, 115, 152
Shams al-Din Juvayni, 59, 61
Shaykh ʿAbd al-Rahman, 59, 61
siege engines, 107, 130
Simon Cephas. *See* Peter
Sinjar, 50, 113
Siyah Kuh, 56, 106
Stephen, 74, 92, 115
Stromboli, 67–68
sukur, 56, 94, 112–13, 155
Sultaniyya, 8, 123, 138
sunqur, 92, 155
Sutai Akhtachi, 127–35
Sylvester, Pope, 67
Syria, 5–8, 10, 18–19, 63, 71, 112, 135n303
Syriac language, 55, 83n163

Tabriz, 7–8, 20, 97–98, 101–2, 103n226, 110, 112, 117, 120–22, 124, 151
Talas, 48
tamgha, 99, 155
Tangut, 47, 55, 58n77, 60

Tegüder. *See* Ahmad Tegüder
Thomas, 3, 9, 70, 115
Toghan, 136, 138, 141–46, 150
Tommaso Anfossi, 69
Turks, 1, 14, 18, 37–38, 46n36, 71
Tus, 48
Tuscany, 76
Tyrrhenian Sea, 67

Ujan, 103, 112, 117, 119, 122–23
University of Paris, 2, 78
Urmia, 32, 61, 106n232, 122n267, 123n271
Ushnuviya, 122

Vakyarud. *See* Jaghatu
volcano, 67–68

waqf, 92, 116, 122, 138, 152, 155
White Feast, 30, 118

yāghī, 127, 129, 133, 136, 146, 155
yarligh, 57, 63, 122, 155
Yoshmut, 59–60

Zayn al-Din Balu, 124, 141
Zion, monastery of, 48
zunnār, 15, 111